i

MODERN
MOONSHINE
TECHNIQUES

34 illustrations
4 flow charts

White Mule Press
Box 577
Hayward, CA 94541

ISBN 978-0-9824055-3-6

www.distilling.com
www.moonshineform.com

Contributors: Tom Hubuck of "Toms Foolery" Chagin Falls, OH;
Jim Blansit, Copper Run Distillery, MO; Alan Dikty, journalist, Chicago, IL;
Eric Watson, Cayman Islands; Dave Thomas, Golden CO;
Rob Masters, Colorado Pure Distilling; and Bill Smith, Treasure Island Distillery.

Edited, with Q&A, by Nancy Fraley; artwork by Catherine Ryan;
book design by Gail Sands, Sebastopol, CA;
Editor, Matthew Rowley
cover photo by Bill Dowd.

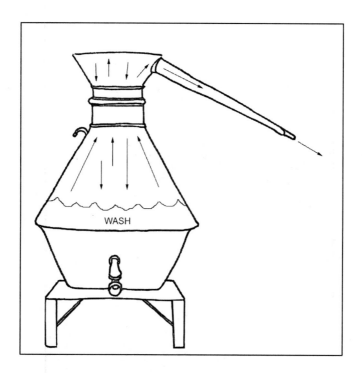

Distillation

Alcoholic distillation is the process of separating ethanol from a fermented wash by evaporation. The vapors are driven off by heat and then collected, condensed and recovered as a liquid. This liquid may also be redistilled to raise its alcohol concentration.

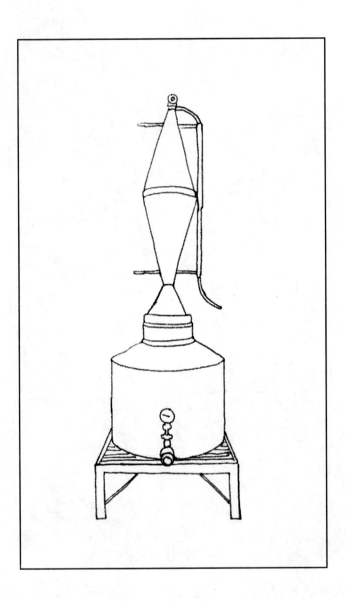

Table of Contents

Distilling Glossary

ABV Alcohol by Volume, often expressed as a percentage (e.g 60% abv).

Aldehyde A volatile impurity found in the foreshots.

BAM: Beverage Alcohol Manual

Barrel Whiskey (wooden) 53 US gallons, 44 Imperial gallons, or 200.6 liters.

Beer Barrel (Stainless Steel) Bbl. 31 gallons.

Beer Stripping A crude primary distillation of fermented wash. See "stripping."

Bubble Cups sit over vapor pipes. When rising alcohol vapors hits the cup it is forced down to the rim. At this point evaporation occurs, enriching the vapors.

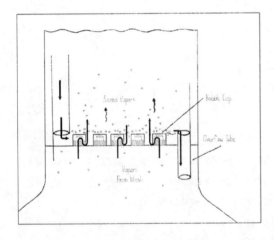

CFR A U.S. government codification of administrative rules, known as the Code of Federal Regulations. Title 27 cover regulations for alcohol beverages.

Charge The volume of alcoholic beverage wash, or low wines going to the still.

Condenser An apparatus, often a "tube in shell," in which hot vapors are cooled and condensed into liquids.

Congeners Impurities. These minor chemicals give liquor (spirits) distinctive character and flavors. They are found in both heads and tails. May be considered desireable or undesireable depending on quantity and type.

Cuts The process of separating different types of alcohol through the foreshots, heads, hearts and tails cuts made during the final distillation run.

Density Meter Portable device that measures specific gravity, thus allowing the distiller to make precise cuts.

Dephlegmator A small pre-condenser that sends distillate back to the pot. This process increases the reflux and the purity of the spirit.

Dextrose Basic sugar also known as corn sugar. An optional base for distilling moonshine.

DME Dried malt extract. When dissolved in water and fermented, can be distilled.

DSP A federally licensed distillery, known as a Distilled Spirits Plant.

Esters Fermented byproducts made by yeast action that contributes fruity characteristics, aroma, and flavor to the wash.

Enzymes Proteins that assist conversion of starches into sugars that will ferment.

False Bottom In a mash tun the false bottom is a slotted copper pipe, the "slots" of which allow wash to drain while holding back the grain.

Final gravity the density of the was after fermentation. Knowing the original and final gravity of a wash allows you to determine the percentage of alcohol of the wash.

Flocculation The clumping and settling of yeast out of solution, forming a cake-like substance in the bottom of the tank or tub.

Foreshots A small amount of low boiling distillate containing acetone, methanol, and aldehyde volatiles. Catch and discard.

Fusel Oil A bitter oil found in tails. A liquid composed of amy and butyl alcohols.

Heads Spirits from the beginning of the run that contain a high percentage of low boiling alcohols such as aldehydes.

Infrared Thermometer Gun Instant reading thermometer device.

Low Wines The spirits collected from the first distillation.

Mash A mixture of ground malted grains and hot water.

Malt Sprouted dried grains. Malted grains contain enzymes that convert starches into fermentable sugars.

Mash Tun A double-jacketed tank with a false bottom in which hot water and grains are mixed.

NGS Neutral Grain Spirits (190+ proof alcohol). Most often produced from corn. Used by distilling companies around the world for blending to produce vodka, gin and whiskey. It is the workhorse of the commerical distillation industry.

Original gravity The density of the wash before fermentation.

Packing Copper mesh or ½" copper T's used in a still's column to increase the surface area and thus the reflux and quality of the alcohol.

Parrot A device resembling a stylized bird that attaches to the still and floats the hydrometer.

Proof A measurement of alcohol's strength: In the US, proof is twice alcohol content at 60°F. (i.e., 120 proof is 60% abv).

Pitch The process of adding yeast to the wash.

Plates: (or tray) Located horizontally at intervals in a column, often contain bubble caps that enrich the reflux

Reflux Formed when vapors condense and re-vaporize in the column of a still.

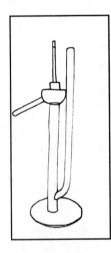

Slop, Hot Hot, stinky, spent corn mash from the still.

Sparging At end of mashing, a process in which hot water is sprayed on, or run through, the grain bed to extract additional sweet barley water.

Spirit Still A still designed to do the final distillation, producing finished whiskey.

Sweet Spot The head temperature between 174°F and 180°F. This range produces a sweet tasting spirit and is considered the heart of the distillation run.

Stripping The process of running low abv wash through a still with no head or tail cuts to remove alcohol that will be re-distilled.

TTB Alcohol and Tobacco Tax and Trade Bureau, formerly BATF.

Tails A distillate containing a high percentage of fusel oil and little alcohol.

Tub A 55-gallon plastic or stainless steel barrel used as a fermentation vessel.

Wash Fermented substrate containing alcohol.

Water Temperature Controller Device that allows cool water to flow through a copper coil, controlling excess heat in a fermentation.

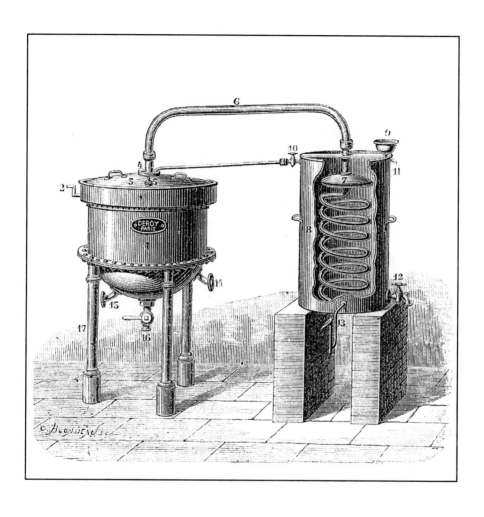

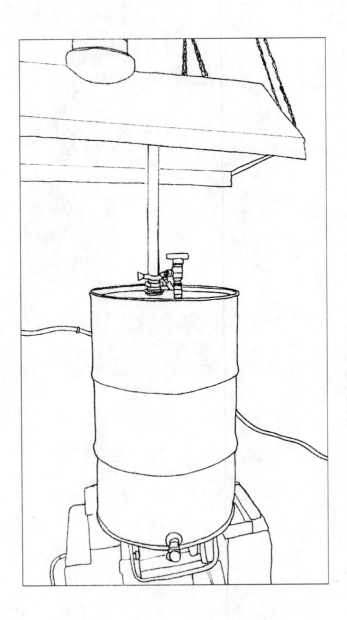

Introduction

Whiskey is simply distilled beer

To learn how to make whiskey you first have to brew beer. Go to ama-zon.com and search "brewing" and you will find numerous books on this subject. The easy way, however, is to take a home brewing class offered at most home brew shops. These shops also sell brewing kits, malt extracts, dried malt extract (DME), malted barley, wheat, rye, and flaked corn.

The next generation of distillers is going to come from the craft brewing industry since they know the complex flavors found in barley make great beer and will make great whiskey.

Modern Moonshine Techniques has three sections: First is how to use sugar to distill a "moonshine." Second, how to build an inexpensive corn cooker and make corn whiskey. Finally, and most importantly, this book, with text and illustrations, shows how to build a mash tun to create a grain whiskey wash. And, then instructions to distill that wash into whiskey.

Finally, get your DSP from the TTB, your State (ABC) license and open an "artisan" distillery. Then distill the grain whiskey here and put it into a barrel. It will, in a matter of months, pick up flavor and color as it matures. And, if you leave your whiskey in a charred oak barrel for two years, it becomes "straight Bourbon whiskey." Craft distilleries often drop the word "straight" and age their whiskey for less than one year.

Bill Owens
White Mule Press
Hayward, CA
USA

Fig. 33. — Soufflet et siphon à air comprimé, pour transvaser les vins, système Vivez.

Chapter 1

Moonshine – The Legend and the Law

"Where the English went, they built a house; where the Germans went, they built a barn; where the Scots-Irish went, they built a whiskey still."

—*An old Appalachian proverb*

With the rise of artisan distillation in the US, most producers have decided to focus on typical spirits such as vodka, gin and rum, or more specialized spirits such as eau de vie or malt whiskey. A few other distillers, however, are choosing to trade on a bit of legendary history and produce moonshine.

The term moonshine was first used in Britain where it referred to employment or other activities that took place late at night. In the US, however, it has always been associated with illegal liquor that has been known under colloquial names such as white lightning, popskull, corn liquor, rotgut, panther's breath, or, more simply, shine.

The practice of moonshining is inextricably tied to US history in numerous ways. After the American Revolution the United States was strapped financially due to fighting a long war. In an attempt to address this problem, a federal tax was levied on spirits. This did not sit well with the newly liberated people who had just concluded a war to eliminate British taxation. This gave rise to the practice of making distilled spirits clandestinely to circumvent taxation.

Early on, this practice was a method of survival, not extra profit. If farmers experienced a bad crop year, they could use their corn for making whiskey. Because this was a practice of subsistence, the payment of tax on this product might mean they would be unable to feed their families. Thus began the contentious relationship with federal agents who often were attacked when they tried to collect the tax.

In 1794, things finally came to a head with the Whiskey Rebellion. A group of several hundred managed to overtake the city of Pittsburgh, Pennsylvania. In reaction, George Washington dispatched 13,000 militiamen to take back the city and jail the leaders. This incident served as the first major test of authority for the fledgling federal government.

The battles between the US Congress and moonshiners continued to rage on. In the 1860s the government attempted to collect more excise taxes to fund the Civil War. In response, a number of elements, including Ku Klux Klansmen, joined the moonshiners in an attempt to fight back. The new alliances led to more brutality and incidents of intimidation of local people who might reveal stills, and revenue of agents and their families.

The Temperance movement then added these happenings to their arsenal on the march towards prohibition. The states began to prohibit the sales of alcohol in the early 1900s, and then complete national prohibition was established in 1920. Prohibition's enactment provided the best possible scenario for moonshiners. With no legal means of obtaining alcohol, demand grew exponentially with which the moonshiners could not keep up. In response, the producers began using cheaper ingredients such as sugar and even watering down their whiskey.

A large network of distribution was established with the assistance of organized crime. To supply the illegal spirits to this network, young men in rural areas close to the still operations delivered moonshine in highly modified, high performance cars. The temptation was irresistible to these men, as the income they could make in a single night was greater that a couple of months of honest work. What started as a transportation method for moonshine gave birth to stock car racing which formalized into today's NASCAR.

With the repeal of prohibition in 1933, the demand for moonshine declined rapidly, returning the practice mostly back to areas concentrated in the Appalachian region of the East Coast. Even today, there is illegal production of moonshine in these regions with operations located in northern Georgia, western South and North Carolina and eastern Tennessee. Due to the independent and strong willed character shared by most Americans, most historians feel that moonshine will always be around in one form or another.

Today there are a few who have decided to produce moonshine legally. Not surprisingly, these individuals are located in the same regions of the East Coast where the illegal version is still made.

WEST VIRGINIA DISTILLING

www.mountainmoonshine.com

West Virginia Distilling is located in a suburb of Morgantown, home to West Virginia University, and is only 8 miles from the Pennsylvania border. The owner and operator of West Virginia's first legal distillery is Peyton Fireman, a lawyer and childhood acquaintance of mine.

Beginning in 1998, Peyton tried to get access to regional, illegal moonshine producers to learn how to make moonshine, but did not have much success. What he found was that the younger generation that he expected to have had the practice of making moonshine handed down to them found that it was far more profitable to grow marijuana than it was to make moonshine. So, he had to learn on his own by reading distilling texts and asking questions of the few microdistillers that existed at the time.

This small distillery is housed in a former transmission shop. Peyton is a very resourceful tinkerer. With the help of a local engineer, he made his stills out of old 40-gallon electric water heaters with columns made from lengths of copper pipe and condensers made from copper coils, all sourced from local home builder supply outlets. He now uses these stills to re-distill head and tail cuts and instead undertakes the main distillation in the equipment pictured above. His total investment to date has only been $40,000! Three times a year, Peyton puts his law practice on hold and becomes a distiller.

Peyton makes only one distillate but it is presented two different ways. One, Mountain Moonshine, is a colorless spirit bottled immediately after final distillation. The other, Old Oak Spirit Whiskey, is mellowed by soaking toasted oak wood chips in it for 30 days.

Peyton introduces corn grits into the home-built still, which also serves as his mash cooker and fermenter. It is heated in a hot water boiler fueled by waste oil that supplies hot water to external coils mounted underneath the vessel. He accomplishes starch conversion by allowing the mash to rest heated for a couple of hours and then adds enzymes.

Once mashing is over, he attaches an external chilling loop to the vessel and cools the mash to fermentation temperature via internal coils. Once cooled, he adds brewing yeast and allows the mash to ferment for 4 to 6 days. When fermentation is over, he then heats the vessel again and distills the alcohol from the wash.

Technically, Peyton is not producing a traditional moonshine but rather a spirit whiskey. His corn mash-derived spirit makes up only 20 percent of his product. To produce the final spirit he blends his distillate with neutral grain spirits. His products are released to market at 80 and 100 proof.

When asked if he feels there is a market for his product, Peyton defers to a quotation from a recent newspaper article. Montie Pavon, the owner of a local bar called Levels, stated "people like the idea of drinking moonshine. They see it up on the shelf and say: 'You sell moonshine? I thought it was illegal.'" This attention-getting feature of the product certainly provides advantages when trying to induce people to try it. Presently, West Virginia Distilling sells a little over 1,000 bottles of Mountain Moonshine and Old Oak Spirit Whiskey per year.

ISAIAH MORGAN DISTILLERY – SUMMERSVILLE, WV
www.kirkwood-wine.com/isaiahmorgan.html

The Isaiah Morgan Distillery is located on the site of the Kirkwood Winery, which was established in 1992 by the late Rodney Facemire. Unlike West Virginia Distilling, this location is tucked into a quiet mountain valley that makes it easy to picture that moonshine has been produced in this region before!

Shirley truly produces his moonshine, Southern Moon, the way it was done in this area for a long time. Instead of mashing milled corn, the raw corn is placed in straining bags and soaked in hot water. The bags are removed after sufficient soaking and cane sugar is added to the liquid left behind. For a still charge of 50 gallons he uses 50 pounds of corn and 100 pounds of sugar. Shirley told us that this practice comes from way back in time where the old timers couldn't mill corn, so they dissolved the husks with lye before soaking the kernels in hot water. No, Shirley does NOT use lye!

The distillery ferments its wash in a group of reclaimed plastic barrels that are connected by a draining manifold that supplies the still.

Shirley charges the still with 50 gallons of wash and conducts a double distillation with the final spirit yield of 7 to 8 gallons at 176 proof. The liquor is then diluted with filtered well water to 80 proof and bottled.

Rodney Facemire can be credited with establishing the classification "mini-distillery" in West Virginia. He managed to get a bill sponsored and passed that created the legal class of alcohol distillers, designated "mini-distillery," which are defined as "where, in any year, twenty thousand gallons or less of alcoholic liquor is manufactured with no less than twenty-five percent of raw products being produced by the owner of the mini-distillery on the premises of that establishment, and no more than twenty-five percent of raw products originating from any source outside this state." Additionally, unlike Wisconsin and some other states, the law allows mini-distilleries permission to allow on-site tasting and on-site retail sales of the liquor they produce. It also allows the mini-distillery to advertise off-site. Because West Virginia Distilling was established prior to this law, it is the only distillery exempt from the ingredient sourcing provision.

In addition to Southern Moon Corn Liquor, Shirley also produces a grappa made from Concord grapes and a rye whiskey. He plans to release a barrel aged version of a whiskey made from rye, malt and corn in 2010. Recently he has begun experimenting with making rum from sorghum molasses pressed from cane grown in Northern West Virginia.

BELMONT FARM DISTILLERY – CULPEPER, VA
www.virginiamoonshine.com

After visiting the Isaiah Morgan Distillery, our trek took us into Southern Virginia about 3 hours southeast of Summersville, West Virginia to Culpeper, Virginia.

Culpeper is a very quiet area of rolling hills with many farms and several well-regarded wineries. The area's quiet appearance belies its close proximity to Washington, DC and Charlottesville, Virginia.

Chuck Miller, owner and distiller, is a consummate showman and quite a character. He opened up his distillery to us which is located in a large converted barn on his farm where he grows all the corn, barley and wheat that goes into his products. If you are a viewer of the History Channel or/and the National Geographic Channel you may have seen him in segments about distilleries.

Chuck produces two products: Virginia Lightning (100 proof) and Kopper Kettle Virginia Whiskey (86 proof). He also sells a version of Virginia Lightning in Japan, but its proof is reduced to 80 to cater to Japanese tastes. Virginia Lightning is made only from corn, whereas Kopper Kettle Virginia Whiskey is produced from corn, barley and wheat. Both are twice distilled.

Unlike Virginia Lightning, which is bottled just after distillation, Kopper Kettle Virginia Whiskey undergoes two stages of wood aging. The first stage exposures the spirit to oak and apple wood chips in a large converted stainless steel dairy tank. After sufficient exposure to the wood in the above tank, it is moved to charred barrels to age for an additional two years before being filtered and bottled. He now sells 4,000 cases per year of his combined product offerings.

Belmont Farm Distillery combines historical and modern equipment. His still, built in 1933, is a mammoth sight to behold and has a capacity of 2,000 gallons.

How Chuck acquired this still is a story in and of itself. It originally was located in New Jersey, where it was operated legally until 1962. The still then was operated illegally until the late 70's when the operation was discovered and shut down by the federal authorities. Just shortly after this, Chuck was beginning to investigate starting his distillery. In a conversation with federal regulators he asked where he might acquire a still for his operation. An agent mentioned that he knew of the still in New Jersey. Shortly thereafter, Chuck negotiated a purchase price and he relocated the still to his farm in Culpeper. Chuck then installed the rest of his equipment and filed for his federal permit in 1980.

Standing in stark contrast to his museum piece still is his elaborate water treatment system that he uses to process water from his on-site well.

Installed on a wall opposite the still room are multi-stage sediment filtration units and a high-capacity deionization unit as well as a reverse osmosis system. We had intended to continue on to North Carolina to visit Piedmont Distillers, the producers of Catdaddy Carolina Moonshine and the recently released Junior Johnson's Midnight Moon, but advance calls to them revealed they were too busy to meet with us. That was unfortunate because had we visited them we would have made a complete sweep of mid-Atlantic and southern producers of legal moonshine and moonshine-inspired products. The most recent resource directory published by The American Distilling Institute and the website ofPiedmont Distilleries does not show them producing a corn whiskey.

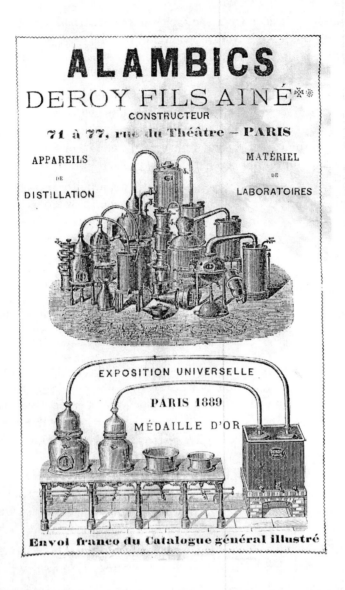

Thanks to Eric Watson for the text on legal moonshiners. He can be reached at: craftbrewfreak@yahoo.com.

Artisan Whiskey Distilleries

Copperfox.biz, Dryflydistilling.com, Stranahanscoloradowhiskey.com, Templetonrye.com, Corsairartisan.com, Peachstreetdistillers.com, Ciscobrewers.com, Montanawhiskey.com, Copperrundistilling.com, Tuthilltown.com, Garrisonbros.com, Highwestdistillery.com, StGeorgespirits.com, Clearcreek.com, Yellowstone Valley Distilling, Solas Distillery, to name a few.

Q&A   The Legend and the Law

1. In the United States, moonshine has always been associated with:

　[a] The production of illegal liquor.

　[b] Employment or other activities which occurred at night.

　[c] A rare kind of lunar eclipse.

2. Common themes running through the practice of moonshining in US history are:

　[a] The avoidance of paying a federal tax, which is normally levied on all spirits.

　[b] Moonshining as a way of making a living in depressed economic conditions.

　[c] An expression of the fiercely independent spirit of the American people.

　[d] All of the above.

　[e] None of the above.

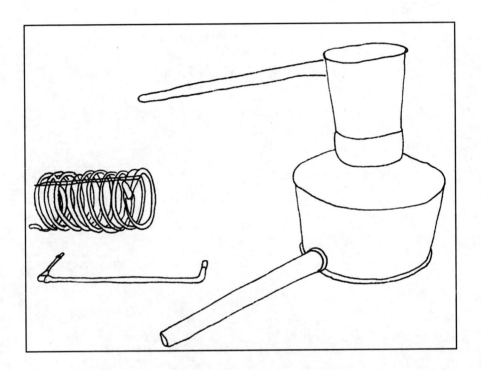

Chapter 2

Distilling in 18th Century America[*]

1.   The corn was first put into a burlap bag and then soaked in a tub of warm water. The water was changed each day for the next three days.

2.   The tub was drained and the corn sat for three more days, or until it sprouted.

3.   The corn was then spread out in the sun to dry.

4.   Once dried, the corn was put back into the bag and tumbled, thus knocking off the sprouts.

5.   The corn was cracked in a roller mill set at 1/64". Flour and corn mills were in every town in America.

6.   The cracked corn was mixed into hot water, thus creating a mash for fermentation. The distiller used the "Rule of Thumb"[**] to determine if the water was hot enough. If he could hold his thumb in the water for 5 seconds it was the right temperature to create the mash.

7.   After mixing, the mash was left to sit for a few hours. This allowed the corn starches to convert to sugars. Some distillers would let the mash just sit and undergo a spontaneous 7-15 day fermentation.

8.   Fermented wash was then bucketed into the still. Today, distillers use a sump pump to move the wash.

9.   The wash was brought up to low boil, allowing vapors to flow up and out to the condenser and the collection pail.

10.   18th Century distillers use smell and taste to distill moonshine.

[Notes: A primitive pot with a 5% abv wash will yield about 25% abv. Moonshiners often double distilled to obtain 100 proof spirits, which was perfect for drinking and bartering for goods and services.]

[*] This is a best effort to figure out how 18th Century distillers made moonshine. How accurate the process is yet to be determined.

[**] The original meaning of the rule word was, you couldn't beat you wife with a stick bigger than you thumb.

Q&A DISTILLING IN 18TH CENTURY AMERICA

1. When distillers in early America used the "Rule of Thumb," it referred to:

   [a] A law which required that all distillers have at least one thumb if they were going to operate a pot still safely.

   [b] A method for determining if the mash of corn and water was hot enough for proper fermentation.

   [c] A method for determining the amount of yeast to use in their whiskey recipe.

2. In order to make all the right heads, hearts, and tails cuts in their distillate, 18th century distillers would:

   [a] Use a very primitive version of modern hydrometers and alcoholmeters.

   [b] Only use their sense of smell and taste.

   [c] Run three or four distillations, thereby coming out with a pure spirit.

3. After the corn was soaked in a tub of warm water, drained, and then spread out to dry, early distillers would then:

   [a] Add more water and immediately distill it.

   [b] Turn it into feed for farm animals.

   [c] Put the corn back into a bag and tumble it, thus knocking off the sprouts.

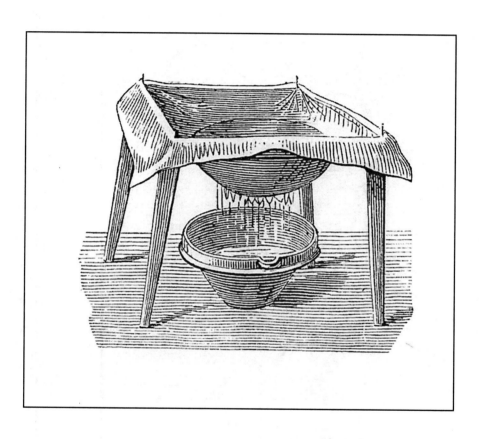

Fig. 61. Still with cooler, MATTHIOLUS

Chapter 3

What's Moonshine?*
Distilled spirits made in an unlicensed still.

Moonshiners don't have a distilling license, and they don't care about government rules. They buy sugar from wholesale vendors such as Costco because a 50 lb. bag of sugar will make about $800 worth of moonshine, and it's easy to make. Some moonshiners just add some whole corn kernels to the sugar wash. When asked why they add corn? They say it adds "flavor." Purists say true moonshine has to be made from corn. Others say moonshine has no definition (under the law) and be made from sugar, fruit, or any grain. Most distillers, however, feel that true moonshine has to be made from 100 percent malted corn.

The only true definition of moonshine is that it's untaxed liquor from an unregistered still. Anything that calls itself moonshine and sits on the self of a liquor store is something else. You hope what you are buying is an un-aged whiskey. Check the website and see if they have pot still. A photo is worth 10,000 words. Several craft distilleries produce moonshine-inspired products on pot stills classified as a "Distilled Spirits Specialty." This CFR classification allows them us use a variety of ingredients to produce "moonshine" that can be sold in liquor stores.

Most people think of moonshine is distilled in the mountains of Kentucky or Tennessee. The truth of the matter is that most commercial brands of bottled moonshines are made from neutral grain spirits (NGS), which is 190 proof spirit. NGS is distilled from corn on gigantic column stills. The two biggest producers of NGS are Archer Daniels Midland Co., (ADM), Decatur, Illinois and MGP in Atchison, Kansas. These companies are the workhorses of the spirits industry producing 90% of the vodka and gin in America. The quality of their products is beyond reproach. Question: what is the difference between NGS produced at an industrial distillery and an artisan distiller? Answer: at 192 proof who cares? Why do distilling companies use NGS? It's cheap source of alcohol and gives you bang for your buck. When you buy a bottle of commercial moonshine what you getting is closer to vodka than an un-aged corn whiskey from an artisan pot still. Look for the real thing by reading the label.

---

*The Spirit Beverage Alcohol Manual (BAM) is a condensed version of the CFRs at 27CFR5.22, Standards of Identity. When designing a product, be careful to read the CFRs; do not depend entirely upon the BAM. www.ttb.gov/spirits/bam.shtml.

The Code of Federal Regulations (CFR) that regulates liquor production in the US defines "Classes" and "Types" for all spirit products. These Standards of Identity (27CFR5.22) do not limit the products that may be made; they simply define the standards under which the identifying term may be used. The overall "Class" called Whiskey is a spirit distilled from a fermented mash of grain at less than 190 proof and bottled at 80 proof or higher.

The Bourbon type is an internationally reserved name for a whiskey made in the US from a fermented mash made from 51 percent or more of corn and stored in charred new oak containers. The length of time required for storage is not defined, nor is the species of oak or its country of origin. This gives artisan distillers broad latitude in choices for their Bourbon products. Have you tasted Bourbon put-up in French Oak? Perhaps that's worth a try; it's only a stone's throw away from a moonshine recipe.

Several other types of whiskeys are defined in the CFRs—like Rye and Wheat—along with modifiers "straight," "light," or "blended." These terms are in the Beverage Alcohol Manual (BAM) for spirits which define 36 different types within the class called Whiskey. None of them is Moonshine.

Merriam-Webster.com defines moonshine as illegally distilled corn whiskey. That's what the encyclopedia and dictionaries say, but that's not what the law (TTB) says. US law does not define the term "moonshine" so that term may not be used as a Class or Type identifier, but that does not rule out the use of "moonshine" as part of a brand name or a so-called fanciful name on a legally produced product. Again, unless the product exactly fits one of the descriptions found in the Standards of Identity, it is likely that the bottle will carry the words "Spirits from Grain" just like most vodka. That being the case, adherence to some legendary formula or recipe is meaningless, so the modern-day moonshiner should exercise his liberty to express himself by creating a unique product that tastes as he likes it.

Learn more by reading the DSP regulations: www.ttb.gov/spirits/spirits_regs.shtml.

Q&A WHAT'S MOONSHINE?

1. According to the Code of Federal Regulations' (CFR) definition for Bourbon, a creative artisan distiller could potentially:

    [a] Use any kind of oak for aging, just as long as the barrel is lightly toasted.

    [b] Age the Bourbon in a French oak barrel that has previously been used for cognac.

    [c] Only use American oak, but choose between old or new barrels for aging.

    [d] Use Hungarian oak if he or she decides to, as long as the oak is both new and charred.

2. The federal Beverage Alcohol Manual (BAM) defines moonshine as:

    [a] Nothing, because U.S. law does not define the term "moonshine" at all.

    [b] Illegally distilled corn whiskey.

    [c] Neutral grain spirits (NGS) mixed with at least 80 percent corn.

    [d] A un-aged 100 percent corn whiskey.

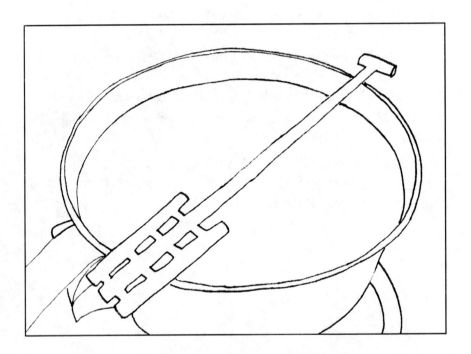

Chapter 4

Moonshine: The Easy Way from Sugar*

American moonshine was traditionally made from corn using a pot still. Moonshiners built their own stills and did not own a thermometer. They distilled by taste and smell alone, and by the "light of the moon," hence the word, "moonshine." This method of distilling, at its best, was primitive and the spirits they created were illegal and still are illegal.

For many generations moonshine was the source of income for poor farmers who distilled as cheaply as possible. Over time, moonshiners started to add sugar to the corn mash because sugar increased the volume of the moonshine. Today, you can purchase a 50-pound bag of sugar for $25.00 from Costco, from which you can make about $800 worth of moonshine. Sugar is still the cheapest ingredient for making moonshine.* If fermented and distilled properly, sugar can make a nice tasting spirit.

There is very little character in a moonshine made from sugar. So, why do moonshiners continue to add corn to the sugar mash? They'll tell you, "It adds to the flavor." Often they use the corn several times—"until the flavor runs out," they explain. In reality, the corn is only adding romance because the corn starches have not been converted to sugars that ferment. Let's be serious about what they're distilling—it's really a high proof "rot gut" rum. There are many books and websites that explain how to ferment sugar to make moonshine because it easy to do. They don't explain how to create a "real" corn mash because making real corn whiskey is a complex process that takes a corn cooker and skilled distiller. That's too much work for the moonshiner who can buy sugar at wholesale prices.

*The purists say moonshine can't be made from sugar. It has to be made from corn.

Q&A MOONSHINE:
THE EASY WAY FROM SUGAR

1. Moonshiners add sugar to moonshine because:

    [a] It greatly increases the volume of the moonshine.

    [b] Is an extremely cheap way to make moonshine.

    [c] Fermenting and distilling sugar did not take a lot of skill on the part of the distiller.

    [d] None of the above.

    [e] All of the above.

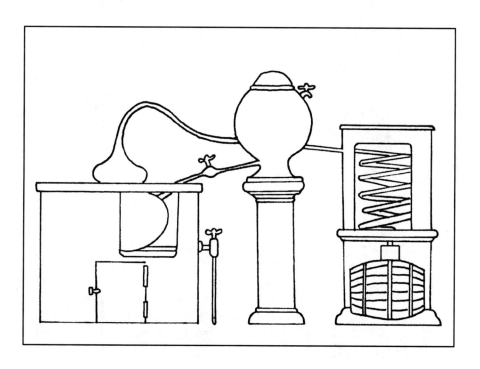

MOONSHINE FROM SUGAR

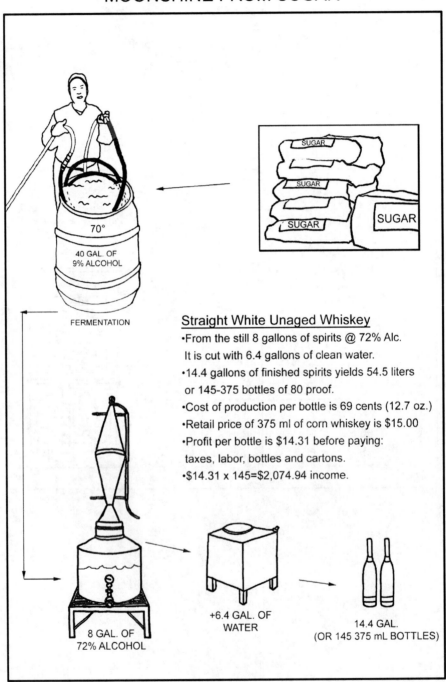

70°

40 GAL. OF
9% ALCOHOL

SUGAR
SUGAR
SUGAR
SUGAR

FERMENTATION

Straight White Unaged Whiskey
•From the still 8 gallons of spirits @ 72% Alc.
It is cut with 6.4 gallons of clean water.
•14.4 gallons of finished spirits yields 54.5 liters
or 145-375 bottles of 80 proof.
•Cost of production per bottle is 69 cents (12.7 oz.)
•Retail price of 375 ml of corn whiskey is $15.00
•Profit per bottle is $14.31 before paying:
taxes, labor, bottles and cartons.
•$14.31 x 145=$2,074.94 income.

8 GAL. OF
72% ALCOHOL

+6.4 GAL. OF
WATER

14.4 GAL.
(OR 145 375 mL BOTTLES)

Chapter 5

How to Distill Moonshine From Sugar

YOU WILL NEED

- Infrared thermometer gun (www.Amazon.com)
- Wooden paddle (canoe or home made)
- Three 55-gallon food grade drums (www.baylesscontainers.com)
- Sump pump and 1" hoses (Home Depot)
- ¾-inch soft copper tubing (local plumbing supply store)
- Hydrometers & alcoholmeter (home brew stores)
- Glass carboys, stainless steel collection pails, or stock pot

THE WISH LIST

- Parrot, in which to float the hydrometer
- Anton-Parr density meter MDA 35N (www.anton-parr.com)
- Used 40 gallon Groen or double-jacketed milk tank (junk yard)
- 55-gallon stainless steel drum turn into a fermentation tank
- Pump, Dayton 2P390A (Grainger.com)
- Count-down digital timer (www.Amazon.com)
- Wash temperature controller (see page 46)

FERMENTATION

- Mix 50 lbs. of sugar into 40 gallons of water.

Predict your original gravity (O.G.) from corn sugar. *1 lb. of corn sugar in 1 gallon of water will give you a O.G. of 1.039.* Take 50 lbs. of sugar and mix it into 40 gallons of water. (50x39/40=48.75). Round up to 1.049. It will ferment out to 1.000 giving you 6% abv. sugar wash. Single pass on a pot still will yield about 8 gallons of 30% abv alcohol spirit.

The Process

Use a sump pump or bail to transfer the wash into the still, leaving behind as much sediment as possible. Turn on the burner to the still and relax as it will take about 30-45 minutes to bring the wash up to temperature. Pure alcohol boils at 173°F, but a 10 to 14% abv wash will boil at a much higher temperature—a little over 190°F. Most kettles don't have a thermometer to monitor wash temperature, only vapor temperature at the still head. This is unfortunate because the still head may not heat quickly, and many a boil-over has happened because the operator did not listen to the sound of the kettle. The sizzle can be heard before full boiling occurs, though it may be difficult to hear over the roar of the burner. Turn the burner down to listen, then back up.

Watch the thermometer on the head of the still. *When the needle hits 160°F, turn down the heat and turn on the water to the condenser.* The still will recover, the temperature will rise, and after a few minutes the distillate will start to spit and sputter as it comes out of the condenser. Have the collection pail (jar) or pot ready. The first sputters from the still are the foreshots. Cut about ½ cup and use it as solvent to clean auto parts.

At 174°F the sputter of distillate from the condenser turns into a small stream. As the still runs, record the distillate temperature, percent of alcohol and time since starting. Collect the distillate in small jars as you learn. Smell and taste what's coming out of the still as the temperature rises. By collecting in small jars, any mistake will not ruin a large quantity of spirit. You will be able to go back and re-sample the jars and get a time-series understanding of what the still is doing. Once you decide where the hearts begin and end, you can combine those jars into a larger container and discard or re-distill the rest. The point is to go slowly and keep records. This avoids making the same mistakes twice, and you will make mistakes.

A 40-gallon wash on a single pass through a simple pot still should yield 10 gallons of hearts at 100 proof alcohol. Let's call it a "spirit" whiskey.

How fast the still flows will depend on several factors:

- The amount of wash
- The amount of alcohol in the wash
- The amount of heat that is being applied to the still
- Size of the condenser

Foreshots: Collect the first ½ cup of distillate. It smells awful. Discard. The amount of foreshots depends upon the quality of the wash.

Heads: Between 175°F to 195°F. Often distillers collect a generous amount of foreshots, skip the heads, and switch to hearts.

Hearts: Between 196°F to 201°F collect 13 gallons. The run starts at 80% abv and is stopped at 20% abv. The 13 gallons should contain 50% abv.

Tails: Don't collect above 203°F. Tails have undesirable oils and esters. Some argue there is a lot of flavor (congeners) in the tails and try to get everything out of them. A hydrometer will tell you how much alcohol is coming out of the still. Do not collect below 20% abv. (Many whiskey distillery stop at 40% abv. A hydrometer reading will tell you when to cut.) Collect the tails in a separate container for a future run. At 20% abv in the distillate, the kettle contains only about 1.5 percent remaining alcohol. You have to determine whether your time and the cost of energy are worth the effort to recover this small amount of alcohol.

[Notes on distilling: At the end of a run the alcohol coming from the still has dropped and water is "picked-up" as the boiling point goes higher. A small pot still will have temperature "spikes" in the head. These spikes create fruit and spice like vapors such as anise and banana. You can taste and smell these flavors. Cut and toss them.]

Double Distillation

Fermentation: Go back to the fermentation process and make two more 40 gallon fermentations. You now have 120 gallons of 14% abv wash for stripping.

Stripping: Using the 120 gallons of wash make three fast stripping runs (don't make head or tails cuts). From each run collect 15 gallons of 100 proof (3x15=45 gallons) in preparation for the final spirits run or "double distillation."

Double Distillation: Into the still add the 45 gallons of 100 proof from the stripping run for the final distillation (where heads and tails will be cut). The final spirit run should yield 15 gallons of 140 proof. Adjust with distilled or RO water to 80 proof for bottling.

[Note: Many distillers add a generous amount of water to the second run, extending the length of the run, making it easier to make more precise cuts.]

Barreling

Barrel age your spirit in a bonded shed or barn, as a wooden building gives a good summer and winter temperature variations. It is the temperature changes that aid in the maturation process. Finally, using 'good' clean water, cut the whiskey to 40% abv or 80 proof. You could also consider using oak chips to give color and flavor to the whiskey, though this may require disclosure on your label.

Profit from Sugar Wash Moonshine

It's cheap to make and distill.

- 90 lbs. of sugar at Costco is $59, yeast $17, water, $5, and labor $30
- Total cost or raw material is $111
- Fermentation producing 40 gallons of wash containing 14 abv
- The hearts run (yield) from the still will be 13 gallons of 50 abv
- Now, add 3.25 gallons of water to the 50 abv, making it 16.25 gallons of 40% abv (80 proof) for bottling, making 5x16.25=81 bottles (750 ml)
- $16/bottle x 81 bottles = $1,300 gross revenue. Bottles sell for $25 at retail.
- Raw cost of ingredients (sugar and yeast) per bottle is $111/107 = $1.37
- Bottle, label, cap, capsule, and carton will add $2.50, raw cost of about $3.90
- $16 wholesale - $3.90 cost is $12.10 margin per bottle
- Now pay CA and US excise taxes - $2.80 /16 =17.5 percent (against wholesale)
- The $12.10 margin – $2.80 tax = $9.30 x 81 = $750 net from distilling a sugar wash

Barrel Aging (increases profitability)

- 6 months, assume angel share of .25 gallons. A dry climate increases abv.
- 12 gallons of spirit @ 50.5 percent cut with 2 gallons of water to get 40 percent alcohol producing 70 bottles.
- Retail price of $35, wholesale of $23 minus bottle & tax of $6.30 = $16.70 $16.70 x 70 = $1,169 net from the distilling run

Other Considerations:

- Federal excise tax: 750ml @ 40 % abv is $2.16 per bottle.
- State tax: varies by state (CA is $0.66).
- Bottle cost: Simple paper label on an inexpensive bottle including closure and tamper evidence, add $3.50.
- Cost of 30 gallon char barrel is about $250. This cost needs to be factored into the above numbers, but barrel can be re-used or sold.
- Factor in the cost of waiting 6 months.
- Aging takes time but adds real value to the product.
- Don't forget: Marketing costs and added channel costs in many states.

Good Luck!

[Notes: What you have distilled is not corn whiskey, which, by law, has to be made from at least 80 percent corn grains. A sugar wash is what TTB calls "a spirit specialty." The label on the bottle can look like it's from the "back woods" but the label has to state it is a "spirit specialty." Some distilleries buy NGS "made from corn" and blend it with their sugar spirit. NGS is cheap and sugar wash is cheap. As stated "moonshine," made from sugar is cheap to produce and has a good profit margin.]

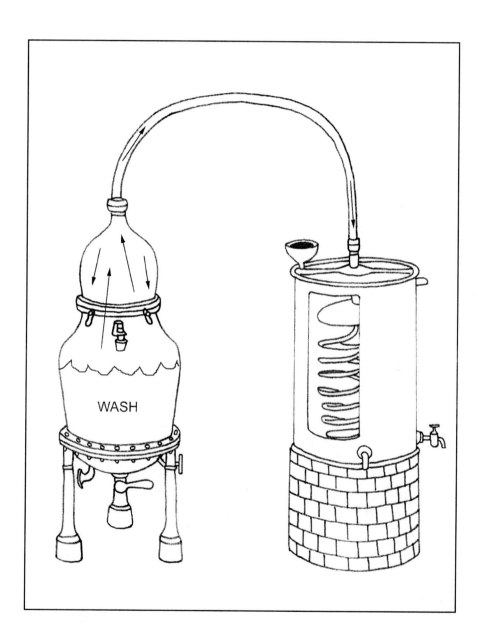

WASH

Q&A HOW TO DISTILL FROM SUGAR

1. When the thermometer on the still head hits 174°F and you begin to see a small stream of liquid coming from the condenser, you should then:

    [a] Smell and taste what is coming out of the still as the temperature continues to rise.

    [b] Record the distillate temperature, abv, and the time since starting distillation.

    [c] Collect the distillate in small jars so you can go back and re-sample them in order to understand what the still is doing over time.

    [d] All of the above.

    [e] None of the above.

2. A 40-gallon wash on a single pass through a simple pot still should yield 10 gallons of hearts at 150 proof alcohol.

    [a] True

    [b] False

3. Circle the correct statement regarding the collection of the hearts:

    [a] They should be collected between 175°F to 195°F.

    [b] You will end up with 27 gallons of hearts.

    [c] The run starts at 80% abv and is stopped at 20% abv.

    [d] The hearts should contain 80% abv.

4. At the end of a run:

    [a] The alcohol coming from the still increases as the boiling point goes higher.

    [b] The alcohol coming from the still decreases and water is "picked-up" as the boiling point goes higher.

5. If you intend to do a double distillation, it would be best for you to:

    [a] Begin the second distillation with the 25 percent low wines from the stripping runs and make the heads, heart and tails cuts during that time.

    [b] Go ahead and make your cuts as you are running through the first 3 stripping runs.

    [c] Not make any cuts at all during the stripping run or the second run.

6. If you intend to age your spirit in barrels, you should keep in mind that:

> [a] In a dry and warm climate, neither the alcohol content nor the overall volume of liquid will be affected during maturation.

> [b] In a dry and warm climate, the alcohol content will drop, while the overall volume of liquid will remain fairly constant.

> [c] In a dry and warm climate, the alcohol content will remain the same while the overall volume of liquid will decrease.

7. The legal definition of the product you will have just distilled is called:

> [a] Moonshine

> [b] A Specialty Spirit

> [c] Corn Whiskey

> [d] Rot-gut

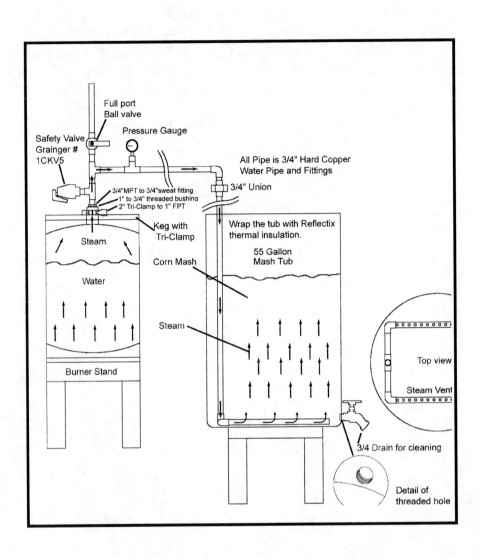

Full port
Ball valve

Pressure Gauge

Safety Valve
Grainger #
1CKV5

All Pipe is 3/4" Hard Copper
Water Pipe and Fittings

3/4"MPT to 3/4"sweat fitting
1" to 3/4" threaded bushing
2" Tri-Clamp to 1" FPT

3/4" Union

Keg with
Tri-Clamp

Wrap the tub with Reflectix
thermal insulation.

Steam

55 Gallon
Mash Tub

Water

Corn Mash

Steam

Top view

Steam Vent

Burner Stand

3/4 Drain for cleaning

Detail of
threaded hole

CHAPTER 6

Building a Corn Cooker

To make real moonshine, use corn. It is inexpensive and a good source of starches that can be converted to sugars for fermentation. Corn has a better flavor than sugar (A sugar fermentation is really producing a rum.) Distillers must have a "corn cooker" to break down the corn starches and most distillers add sugar to the mash to get higher gravity and thus produce a stronger spirit. A straight corn mash yields about 6% abv and a sugar bump (50 lbs. corn and 50 lbs. of sugar will give you 9% alcohol). So, here is how you build a corn cooker.

EQUIPMENT TO BUILD A CORN COOKER

- One 15.5-gallon beer keg fit it with a 2" tri-clamp to 1" FTP. Connect the 2" tri-clamp ferrule to keg with an O-ring attached to the tri-clamp = the keg (no welding necessary).
- One 55-gallon food-grade plastic drum, called the "tub"
- One custom-made steam pipe fitted with a ball and pressure valves
- One safety valve (Granger.com, item # 1C2V5)
- One 50' roll of 3/4" "L-Soft" copper tubing. The copper tubing is available at your local plumbing supply store. Now build a coil heat exchanger by cutting the tubing to 40' and roll it into a coil (see illustration).

THE WISH LIST

- A 2" flexible impeller mash pump (to move mash to the still)
- Infrared thermometer gun
- 100 gallon double jacket tank
- One "Groen" soup kettle
- One 600-micron Ez Strainer (USPlastic.com/catalog)
- One large mash pump
- One electric gear drive tank mixer for blending low-viscosity materials
- One pump, Dayton 2P390A (Grainger.com or surpluscenter.com)

INGREDIENTS

- 50 gallons of water
- 50 lbs. cracked corn from a feed and seed store
- 20 oz. Turbo yeast
- 25 lbs. malted barley

This makes 40 gallons of 6% abv wash for one distillation.

PROCEDURE

Overnight: Soak 50 lbs. of cracked corn in a tub of hot water. The next day, drain the tub.

Day Two: Repeat the process.

Day Three: Repeat the process.

[If you are planning to double distill, use three tubs, repeating the process above to create 120 gallons of wash.]

COOKING THE CORN

1. Set up the cooker (See illustration pg. 28) by inserting the steam pipe into the wash tub, making sure that it does not touch the bottom. Now add 40 gallons of fresh water to the tub. Turn on the steam and start heating the water before adding the corn.

Mix 15 lbs of the crushed malted barley into the corn. (This small amount of barley keeps the corn from becoming a thick porridge). Now, add the mixture to the mash tub. As the mash heats up and cooks the corn will gelatinize, making it difficult to stir. If necessary, add more water to mixture. An electric gear tank mixer (agitator) will make this job easier. It can take a few hours to bring it up to 212°F.

Note: The mash water needs to be at least 15 ppm calcium and almost devoid of iron. The pH should also be adjusted to about 6.0 (Most city water is 8-9 pH.) Not adjusting pH is the biggest reason mashes fail.

2. Use caution and do NOT rush the cooking process as you are pushing live steam through a thick mash. This is not for beginners.

3. Cook the mash for 1 hour, then turn off the steam system. Allow the copper pipe to cool. Use gloves to remove the steam pipe.

4. Insert the copper "coil" heat exchanger into the mash. If you don't have a coil, you will have to wait hours for the mash to cool. When the mash has cooled to 152°F, remove the coil and use a wooden paddle stirring in 20 lbs. of malted barley to the wash. Again, the easy way to mix the mash is with an electric, gear drive tank mixer. Mixing in the barley malt will cool the mash another 10°F, to around 145°F.

At 145°F to 155°F barley enzymes will convert corn mash to a sugar wash. Don't worry about the starch conversion temperature. If it is between 130°F and 160°F conversion will happen because American 2-row barley has a lot of enzymes. (Keep the agitator running during starch conversion).

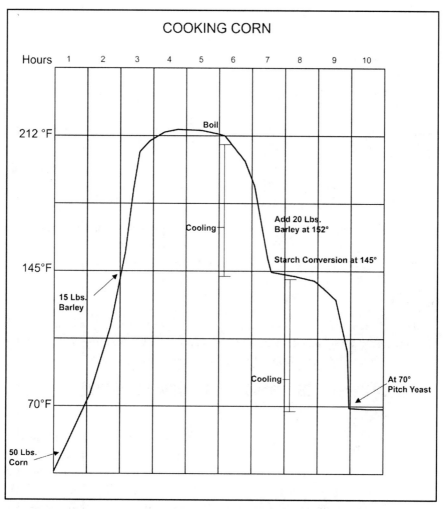

COOKING CORN

5. It takes over an hour for starch conversion to occur. Now for the second time, insert the cooling coil back into the wash, or just wait several hours for it to cool down. Many distillers wait over night for the mash to cool. This is not a good practice. Cool the mash from 143°F to 70°F. At 70°F pitch the yeast.

6. Use the infrared thermometer gun to double check the temperature of the wash. At 70°F "pitch", or mix in, 20 oz. of Turbo yeast. At this point oxygenate the mash by bubbling air through it. (Use a large aquarium pump)

It you don't oxygenate the mash, it will start to ferment and then stop around 1.030 (gravity).

7. The wash will take between 5 to 10 days to ferment. Remember, as the wash ferments it will heat up. The goal here is to "hold" the fermentation below 75°F. High temperature fermentations produce off flavors that come through during distillation.

8. When fermentation is finished, there will be no more bubbles.

9. If using a plastic drum as a fermentation tank use a sump pump to move the wash into the still. In order to get the last five gallons of liquid out it will be necessary to tip the tank. Drain the liquid through a Ez Strainer, leaving behind the corn pulp. This liquid, which is about 5 gallons, goes into the still.

Note: Remember never pump corn solids into a direct fired still it should be strained to keep out solids.

10. Keep two log books: one on cooking and fermentation of the wash, the other log for distillation. It is very important to keep records so that you do not make the same mistakes twice.

11. Distill the wash. Make a fast run stripping alcohol from the wash to produce a low wine of 25% alcohol. Distill the low wine a second time (double distillation) in order to get moonshine that is 65% abv.

12. Clean up the mess. (Do not drink while driving a car or distilling alcohol).

Note: With everything said and done and you insist on distilling corn whiskey do it the easy way using pregelatinized precooked corn. Take a brewing class and learn how to make wash from precooked corn. The recipe is 80% corn, 20% barley.

DISTILLATION OF CORN WHISKEY (USING A POT STILL)

Here is how.

The yield from fermentation of a corn mash is 5% abv. Distilling this mash on a "primitive" pot still (without packing) will yield about 25% abv. [*To get 80% abv on a single run requires having alcohol wash of 8 to 10% abv and a still with packing mesh or plates.*] Many moonshine distillers "double" distill by taking 25% abv from the first run called low wines and distill it a second time yielding 50% abv. (100 proof).

A whiskey distiller often runs into the late (tail) fraction with head temperature reaching 202°F at the high end. When aging whiskey tails are sometimes added back as they "soften" in the oak barrel. Adding tails to a clear moonshine or unaged whiskey is avoided as they contain esters giving the drinker a headache.

DOUBLE DISTILLATION

First run—5% abv low wine becomes 25% abv low wine

- Distill the 40 gallons of wash by making a fast striping run (no heads or tails cuts) collecting 12 gallons of 25% abv.

- Repeat this process three more times, each time collecting 12 gallons from each of 4 runs.

  Total 42 gallons.

Second Run: 25% abv low wine becomes 60% abv.

- Foreshots: Collect and toss the first 4 oz.

- Heads & Hearts: Run together collecting 18 gallons of 60% abv/120 proof.

- Tails: Save tails and add them to the next distillation.

SUMMARY

Cooking corn mash, from start to finish, takes about 5 hours. Fermentation of the mash on average takes about a week. Making corn whiskey from scratch is a lot of work. Distillers do it because of tradition, but, more importantly, because corn is cheap.

The problem with using corn to make whiskey is that it requires two distillations. The first distillation of a 5% abv wash will only yield about 25% alcohol (50 proof). Double distilling the wash produces 50% alcohol or 100 proof. To run a more efficient still, moonshiners use sugar in the fermentation tub.

The most efficient to make whiskey is on a column still (see chapter 11) where is it is easy to get a 100 proof whiskey on the first run. Most distillers learn the distillation process on a pot still before moving up to a column still.

I suggest you make whiskey the modern way by first learning how to brew beer. Your local home brew shop hosts classes how to make "wash" from malt extract and how to use a mash tun to produce a beer wash. To be a whiskey distiller you need to learn how to make wash from malted barley, pre-gelatinized corn flakes, wheat and rye. Most important these beer washes will yield 8-10 % alcohol for distillation.

Why did I devote two chapters of this book to building a corn cooker and distilling moonshine? Because, people prefer to do things the traditional way (often the hard way). It's also the craftsmanship of producing a hand-crafted product. Or, perhaps they just like the "hot" taste of a good corn whiskey.

Finally, if you have a still that is direct fire, I strongly recommend that you filter or strain all of the wash, keeping solids out of the kettle. If corn solids get into the kettle they will burn, producing an off-flavored spirit. If possible, build a still with steam jacket or, better yet, convert an steam jacketed brewing kettle into a still. Again, do not distill the fermented mash unless you have a steam jacketed still!

It is important to separate the grain from the wash before distilling it.

To operate a still you need a federal license known as a DSP permit. So get busy and get your state and federal licenses. And, then you will be welcomed to the industry as an artisan distiller.

To obtain a detailed document titled "Steam Wand Mashing" go to: www.artisan-distiller.net. Special thanks to Sherman Owen of artisan-distiller.net for the information on how to build the corn cooker.

Q&A HOW TO BUILD A CORN COOKER

1. The biggest reason why mashes fail is:

    [a] Because the distiller put too much barley into the mash.

    [b] Because the pH was not adjusted to about 6.0.

    [c] Because the distiller did not mix in enough water to the mash.

2. Around 145°F, barley enzymes will begin to convert corn starch in sugar.

    [a] True

    [b] False

3. After you have pitched the Turbo yeast into the corn mash, you should:

    [a] Walk away and leave the mash alone.

    [b] Oxygenate the mash by bubbling air through it with a large aquarium pump.

    [c] Add 20 lbs. of 2-row malted barley to the mash.

4. Assuming you intend to do a double distillation, you will end up with what percentage of low wine after your first stripping run?

    [a] 65% abv.

    [b] 10% abv

    [c] 25% abv

5. If you have a direct fire still, it is strongly advisable to:

    [a] Get rid of it immediately

    [b] Allow solids into the kettle, so that they will produce interesting flavors like banana or anise.

    [c] Strain or filter the wash so that the solids don't burn and produce off-flavors.

6. Before you can legally operate a still, you must first:

    [a] Obtain your federal DSP (Distilled Spirits Plant) permit, as well as state licenses.

    [b] Practice by making a few trial runs on your still before applying for your permits.

    [c] Operate your still at night under the light of the moon.

    [d] Send the government a sample of the spirit you have produced.

Distilling in 15th Century France

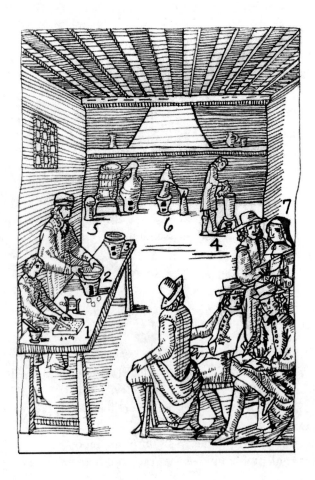

1. Cleaning
2. Seeping
3. Fermentation
4. Cooking
5. Distilling
6. Redistilling
7. Fondling

Chapter 7

I See the Future and it's Whiskey

There are 165 craft distilleries in the US, of which 32 produce whiskey. In the future this segment of the distilling industry will grow quickly because a new generation of distillers has adapted the micro-brewers' technique of creating a wort/wash using a mash tun. This system of separating the grain from the fermentable liquids creates *a bright clean beer wash* without phenol-releasing husks and grains. This is the system of producing distillers' wash that is used by Irish and Scottish distillers.

The new generation of distillers is using malted barley, wheat and rye to create new styles of whiskeys. They shy away from corn because corn mash requires a cooking vessel. Pound for pound, corn produces a thinner wash with lesser flavor. And, extracting sugars from corn requires adding malt for enzymatic action. Making corn whiskey is time consuming.

Many whiskey distillers cook, cool and ferment in the same vessel. Then the wash is pumped directly into the still. This means ⅓ of the wash (in the still) is made up of husks and other undesirables. This cooked corn mash yields about 6% abv and has a potential for off-flavors. *It is important to note that the corn wash has to be quickly removed from the still to avoid "pig slop" aromas in the distillery.*

In contrast, a distillery utilizing a brewer's mash tun with a false bottom doesn't have this problem. The mash tun allows you to drain and cool the grains. Then they are shoveled out into waiting barrels and hauled away expeditiously by a local farmer.

The whiskey distilling process is often done using two stills: a larger pot for stripping, and a smaller spirits still for cutting head and tails. This style of distilling is also done in the brandy and rum industry.

Finally, a whiskey distiller does not need a tall column still with numerous plates. It can be done on a pot still (no plates) or a still equipped with a short column with one or two plates and a dephegmator (pre-condenser).

Which is better? A pot still doing double distillation, or a column still with plates? Both can produce 70% abv/140 proof whiskey for barreling. Column still distillation is faster than pot distillation, and both yield excellent results. The system doesn't matter because whiskey has the magic…it has the buzz.

Q&A I SEE THE FUTURE
AND IT'S WHISKEY

1. Why should artisan whiskey distillers adapt the micro-brewers' technique of creating a wash using a mash tun with a false bottom?

   [a] Because separating the grain creates a bright, clean beer wash without phenol-releasing husks and grains.

   [b] It makes it easier to clean the still, thus avoiding "pig slop" aromas in the distillery and surrounding area if the spent material is not removed quickly.

   [c] Using a false-bottom mash tun to remove husks and other undesirable solids aids in the prevention of off-flavors in the whiskey.

   [d] None of the above.

   [e] All of the above.

2. Below are listed reasons for why the new generation of distillers tends to shy away from the use of corn in producing their whiskeys. Please circle the statement which is NOT true:

   [a] Pound for pound, corn produces a thinner wash than malted barley, wheat, or rye.

   [b] Working with corn means that the distiller must take an extra step to add hydrolytic enzymes from malt, fungus, or bacteria in order to extract sugars.

   [c] Malted barley, wheat, and rye do not require as much water as corn does to produce a mash.

   [d] Corn produces a wash with less alcohol and flavor.

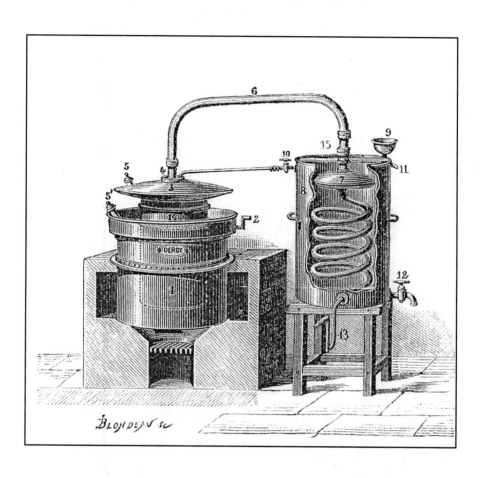

WHISKEY DISTILLING

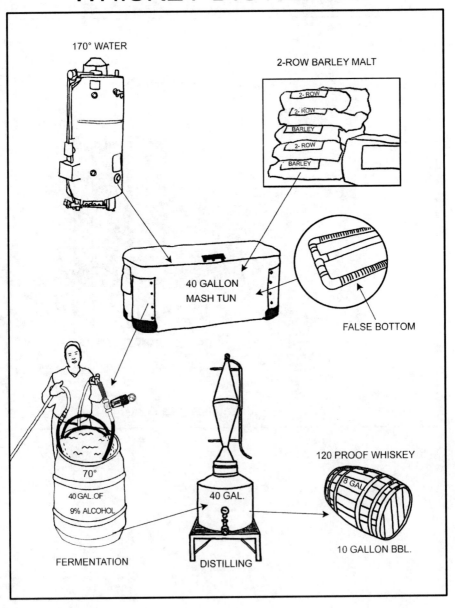

170° WATER

2-ROW BARLEY MALT

2-ROW
2-ROW
BARLEY
2-ROW
BARLEY

40 GALLON
MASH TUN

FALSE BOTTOM

70°

40 GAL.OF
9% ALCOHOL

FERMENTATION

40 GAL.

DISTILLING

120 PROOF WHISKEY

8 GAL.

10 GALLON BBL.

Chapter 8

Building a Mash Tun

Start by purchasing a 50-gallon Coleman camping cooler. Large coolers are also available at Home Depot. In the bottom of the cooler, install the "false bottom." It consists of slotted copper pipes that allow the wash to drain while holding back the grains; hence the term "false bottom."

Materials:

- One 50-gallon camping cooler
- 10" of ⅔" copper pipe and 4-1 elbows, 1-T
- 1" to ½" reducer
- One ½" ball valve (drain)

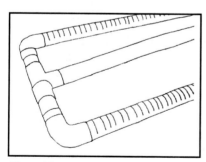

Note: Slots, face down in mash-tun.

Start by cutting the pipe into three sections (two-31" & one- 29"). Take pipe to machine shop or use a hack saw and at every ⅔ of inch, cut slots 40 percent into the pipe (see illustration). Sweat solder the 31' sections together forming a rectangle grid. The 29' pipe is connected to the drain from a T in the center of the back of the grid. Do not solder the T as it connects to the 29" pipe that is connected to a ½" reducer that runs through the drain hole. On the outside of the cooler drain attach the ball valve. The above measurement will depend on the type of cooler you have purchased. Most likely it will be necessary to measure and cut the pipe to fit inside your cooler.

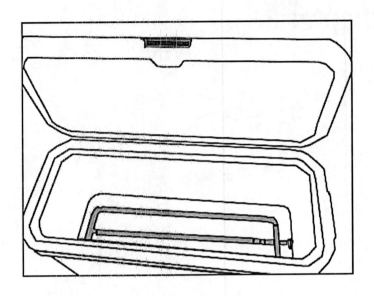

HOW IT WORKS

The Mash Tun: This system uses a 200-quart (50-gallon) camping cooler as a mash tun. It has been fitted with a false bottom that drains the sweet barley water while holding back the grains. A 50-gallon mash tun can hold 30 gallons of water and 125 lbs. of grain. Sparging requires 20 gallons of hot water.

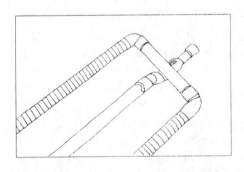

There is little difference in the production of a beer wort and a whiskey wash. Both are created in the mash tun using the simple infusion method of "Time and Temperature." The difference in the process is what happens to sweet barley water after it leaves the mash tun. For the distiller, the barley water goes straight into the fermentation tank where it is cooled and fermented. After fermentation it is called wash and is then distilled into whiskey. *Brewery wort runs into a kettle where it is boiled with the addition of hops. After boiling it is cooled and fermented—and called beer.*

AUXILIARY EQUIPMENT

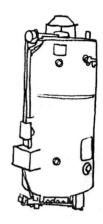

- Commercial water heater (ebay.com)
- Wash temperature controller (www.Grainger.com)
- 50 feet of ¾ L- Soft copper pipe (coiled into heat exchanger)
- Count-down digital timer or iPhone app
- Infrared thermometer gun (www.Testequipmentdepot.com)
- High temperature water pump www.Granger.com item or ebay.com
- Sump pump and hoses for pumping wash to still. (www.grainer.com)
- Wooden paddle (www.Amazon.com)
- Three 55-gallon plastic drums (www.bayleccontainers.com)
- One 55-gallon stainless steel drum (www.surpluscenter.com)
- Anton-Parr density meter DMA 35N (Anton-Paar.com) (Instant specific gravity and alcohol reading)

PROCEDURE: SEVEN STEPS TO CREATE WASH

1. Striking: Adjust the temperature gauge on the water heater to 172°F or use the pot still and heat water to 172°F. Use a high temperature water hose and "strike" by transferring 30 gallons of hot water from the water heater to the mash tun filling it about ¾ full. This water is called the "foundation."

Use the thermometer gun to check temperature of the foundation water. You will notice the water temperature has dropped 10°F to 160°F.

Note, if you are using the still to heat the foundation water, you will have to pump it to the mash tun. Do not bucket it! Pumping hot water is also dangerous. If it splashes on your skin, you will get a serious burn! Use gloves and caution when handling the pump and hoses.

2. Mash-In: Once the foundation water is in the mash-tun, work quickly and add the grains. The grain floats, so use a paddle and mix them into the foundation water. This is called "mashing-in." Stir for one minute or until the mash is lump free. Close the lid to the tun, holding in the heat.

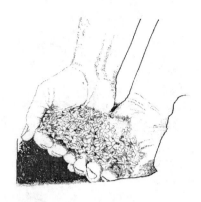

Malted barely, when mixed with hot water, will release enzymes within minutes that convert the starch water into sugar water. Use the thermometer gun to take the mash-in temperature reading for the log book. Mashing-in will also create a temperature loss of 8-10°F. During the mashing-in process, you can expect a temperature loss of 25-30°F. The final temperature of the mash should be around 152°F. A low 130°F or high 160°F mash-in is not a problem. The yields (alcohol) from the wash will be lower. Don't worry about it, just keep going. You won't get it right on the first try.

If you didn't mash-in a perfect 152°F, remember that 2-row barley malt is loaded with enzymes and even with wide temperature variations, it will produce enzymes that convert the starch water to sugar water. Now take a spoon and dip out some of the wash and taste it. I promise it will be sweet. Close the lid to the mash tun to prevent heat loss. *Note, most distillers mash in at 144°F.*

3. Starch Conversion: Set the count-down timer for 40 minutes and walk away. During the 40 minutes, starch conversion will continue.

The mash tuns at micro-breweries hold 2,000-5,000 lbs. of barley. They need to steam-heat the tun and use mechanical rakes to insure a good mash in. The rakes also push the grains out of the tun when sparging has finished. Small brewers stir the mash by hand and use a shovel to dig the grains out the tun.

During the starch conversion period, take the time to write down in the logbook what happened during the mash-in process. This ensures that you don't make the same mistakes twice, and you will make mistakes. This is not a science project. It's a brewing project.

4. Sparge Water: During starch conversion the water heater will have recovered and you again have 170°F water. This water will be used for "rinsing" the grains. If you don't have a water heater, sparge water can be heated in the pot still. You will only need 15 gallons, so heating the water in the pot still will only take a few minutes.

Sparging is a balancing act. Open the valve on the false bottom and start collecting the sweet barley water. Next add the 170°F sparge water to the grain bed covered with water. It can be sprayed.

The balancing act is to add as much water to the mash-tun as sweet water runs out of the bottom.

After a few minutes the mash will begin to settle. Do not mix. Collect 45 gallons of sweet barley water for fermention. After collecting for whiskey mash, keep on collecting the sweet water from the mash tun. It contains sugars from which you can make a small batch of beer.

I suggest a "short sparge" of 15-20 gallons because you want to make a high gravity wash. The more you sparge, the more dilute the wash, giving you less fermentable sugar. Our goal for whiskey wash is 9% abv. A hydrometer reading will give you the potential alcohol for fermentation with a starting gravity of 10.80. *Note: Micro-brewers who make barley wine seldom sparge because they want a create a beer that is 12% abv.*

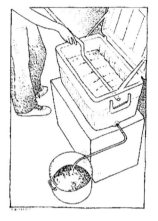

It will take about 30 minutes of sparging to collect 45 gallons for a 40 gallon wash. As 10 gallons of wash will be lost in cooling fermentation and pumping.

Grains sparge differently, and corn is the most difficult to work with. Use rice hulls in the mash to provide a pathway for the sparge water. I suggest your corn whiskey mashes contain 20 percent malted barley and 10 percent rice hulls. The barley will ensure good enzyme action and the rice hulls will create mash that is thin enough to allow the wash to run.

5. Cooling: The 45 gallons of wash has been collected, pumped, or bucketed into the fermentation tank. If possible build a 4-foot platform for the mash tun. This way, the wash from the tun can flow directly into a fermentation tank and there is no need to collect or pump it.

The wash coming into the fermentation tank will be over 100°F. Use the infrared temperature gun to check the temperature of the wash. As soon as the wash starts running to the fermentation tank, insert the copper coil and start cooling.

Pitch the yeast when the wash has cooled to 70°F.

[Note, wineries use flat stainless steel plates to control temperature during fermentation.]

6. Fermentation. Before pitching the yeast, record the original gravity of the wash. A 125 lb. malted barely mash should produce a wash with an O.G. of 1.070. After fermentation the F.G should be 10.10, yielding a wash of 9-10% abv. Again, keep notes so that you can correct any mistakes on the next mash-in. No one gets it right the first time.

In 4 to 6 hours after pitching the yeast, tiny bubbles will appear in the wash. In a few more hours, fermentation will be "rolling" and you will be able to see that the wash is moving around. As the wash ferments, it will give off heat. Use the copper coil to hold the fermentation temperature at 70-75°F. A high-temperature fermentation will create esters in the wash. During distillation, these esters will create off-flavored spirits.

Do not cover the tank with a tight lid. A barley wash fermentation is very active and the foam will push the lid off the tank and onto the floor, making a mess to clean up.

Once fermentation has slowed, you can use a loose lid to cover the tank. Use your eyes and watch fermentation. When the fermentation bubbles have stopped (5-7 days), a bright clean wash can be pumped directly to the still for fermentation. Try to not carry over any yeast into the still.

7. Clean-up: Leave the lid to the mash-tun open for a couple of hours allowing the grain to cool. Leave the false bottom drain open so the grain bed drains.

Once the grain bed has cooled, use a small plastic or wooden shovel and dig it out. Spent grain can be fed to pigs or cows. However, it needs to be cut with 90% commercial animal feed. Cows have multi-chambered stomachs and the sugar in the grains will ferment, bloating and killing the cows. I have heard of pigs getting drunk and killing each other.

WASH TEMPERATURE CONTROLLER

(Grainger.com)

Parts:

1. Solenoid Valve 2 way (#4A700)
2. Solenoid Valve Coil 120 (#A706)
3. Controller PM6C1EHAAAA
4. RTD probe that can be inserted in to the wash
   (Items 3 & 4 at www.instrumart.com)

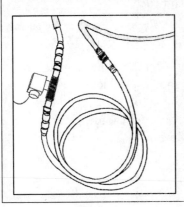

A copper coil equipped with the "regulator" will allow water to flow through the coil and keep a fermenting at wash at 72°F. The coil is a "must" when doing a high gravity sugar fermentation. Without it, heat (90° to 100°F) from the fermentation kills the yeast and yields a stuck fermentation. High temperature fermentations also produce an off-flavored wash.

Several years ago I made some beer and tossed 30 lbs. of spent grain in the backyard. One year later it is still there. Worms won't eat spent grain unless it is cut with green material and composted. It is a lot of work to compost spent grain. If you don't have a farmer to come get the spent grains put them in a bag send them to the dump. This isn't very GREEN but spent grains are hard to recycle. You may to pay to get rid of them

Now, back to the clean-up. After digging out the grains, use a rubber glove to remove the slotted false bottom pipes. They will still be hot, so rinse with cold water and disassemble. No soap or chemicals are necessary, just wipe and air dry everything, including the tun. You can also use heads from a distillation to clean the mash tun. Again use gloves.

Total set-up time to create strike water, mash-in, sparging, pitch yeast, and clean up is about 3 hours.

In about 72 hours, the wash fermentation should be about 70 percent completed. Use the hydrometer to check. The yeast is now starting to flocculate and to settle on the bottom of the tank. It will form a one-inch thick cake slurry and can be collected for the next fermentation. With a final gravity of 1.010 the wash will be almost clear. At this point, drop a sump pump into tank and pump the wash into the pot still. If you're careful, very little yeast will be pumped over.

If you distill on a regular basis you can re-pitch the yeast for numerous batches. Always refrigerate the yeast between fermentations. Yeast is a single-cell organism and it doesn't keep for months without feeding it sugar or fresh wash. Yeast is also cheap. If you just distill once a month, start with fresh yeast on each fermentation.

You are now ready to distill a "single malt" whiskey.

Wash Log Book

Date: Dec 2, 2008

Volume of Distilling Wash: 40 gallons

Type of Wash: Malt Whiskey

Grains: 125 lbs. 2-row malted barely

Strike Water: 35 gallons @ 170°F

Mash-in Temperature: 157°F

Volume of Sparge Water: 10 gallons

Sparge Water Temp: 170°

Original Gravity: 1.068

Yeast Type: Ale yeast, White Labs

Fermentation: 72°

Days of Fermentation: 5 days

Final Gravity: 1.006

Wash Alcohol: 8.1%

Notes (or) wash evaluation _____

_____

_____

_____

_____

_____

_____

Q&A BUILDING A MASH-TUN

1. Circle the statement which most accurately describes the difference between a beer wort and a whiskey wash:

    [a] There is a big difference between a beer wort and a whiskey wash, because, unlike a beer wort, whiskey wash can only be made with wheat, corn, or rye.

    [b] There is little difference, except that when brewery wort leaves the tun, it is then boiled in a kettle, hops are added, and it is then allowed to cool and ferment.

    [c] For the distiller, after the sweet barley water leaves the tun, 20% corn is added in order to increase the complexity and aroma of the wash.

    [d] The only difference is that after fermentation, a distiller's "wash" will then be distilled into whiskey.

2. In creating a wash, a "foundation" can best be described as:

    [a] The water which is first heated in the water heater or pot still and then transferred to the mash tun.

    [b] An endowment or fund established for educational or research purposes in the micro-distilling industry.

    [c] The mixture of malted barley, water, and yeast.

    [d] The real bottom, found below the false bottom of the mash tun.

3. The final temperature of the mash should be around 152°.

    [a] True

    [b] False

4. The term "mashing-in" refers to:

    [a] A British colloquialism for mashed potatoes.

    [b] The process whereby the distiller takes a paddle and then crushes or "mashes" the grain in order to remove the hull.

    [c] The process of quickly adding and then mixing grains into hot water in the mash tun.

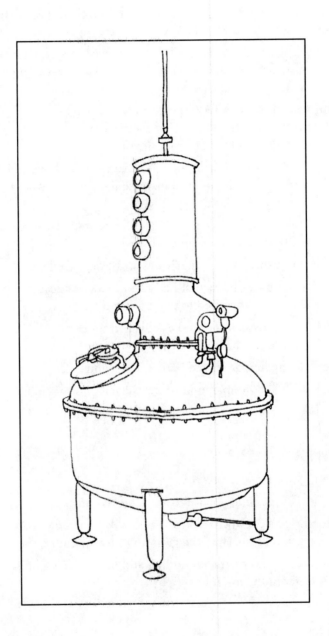

Chapter 9

Whiskey Washes

Whiskey in the US is a spirit of ethyl alcohol distilled from fermented mash of grains. It is not aged but stored in oak barrels. There are no rules or recipes other that the minimum amount of the base material; i.e., made from 51% corn to be Bourbon whiskey or 51% rye to be rye whiskey.

FERMENTATION PRODUCING 40 GALLON PER BATCH:

STRAIGHT BOURBON WHISKEY*

- 60 lbs. of flaked corn
- 55 lbs. of 2-row malted barley
- Mashing time 35 minutes
- Fermentation 7 days
- 40 gallons of 9% abv
- Stripping run at 35% abv
- Spirits run 70% abv
- Barreled at 60% abv/120 proof
- Aged 2 years

BOURBON WHISKEY

- 60 lbs. of flaked corn
- 55 lbs. of 2-row malted barley
- Mashing time 35 minutes
- Fermentation 7 days
- 40 gallons of 9% abv
- Stripping run at 35% abv
- Spirits run 70% abv
- Barreled at 60% abv/120 proof
- Age statement required

*The ingredients for Straight Bourbon Whiskey and Bourbon Whiskeys are exactly the same. (CRF rules). What is different? "Straight" whiskeys have to be stored in charred new American oak barrels for two years.

CORN WHISKEY

- 80 lbs. of flaked corn
- 20 lbs. of 2-row barley malt
- 10 lbs. rice hulls (optional)
- Mashing time 35 minutes
- Fermentation 7 days
- 40 gallons of 8% abv
- Stripping run at 35% abv
- Spirits run 70% abv
- Less than 30 days old

MALT WHISKEY

- 120 lbs. 2-row malted barley
- Mashing time 35 minutes
- Fermentation 7 days
- 40 gallons of 9% abv
- Spirits run 70% abv
- Barreled at 60% abv/120 proof
- Age statement required

RYE WHISKEY

- 61 lbs. of rye
- 59 lbs. of 2-row
- Mashing time 35 minutes
- Fermentation 7 days
- 40 gallons of 9% abv
- Stripping run at 35% abv
- Spirits run 70% abv
- Barreled at 60% abv/120 proof
- Barrel aging statement not required

WHEAT WHISKEY

- 70 lbs. malted wheat
- 53 lbs. 2-row
- Mashing time 35 minutes
- Fermentation 7 days
- 40 gallons of 9% abv
- Stripping run 35% abv
- Spirits run 70% abv
- Barreled at 60% abv/120 proof
- Barrel aging statement not required

The modern craft distiller is using smaller 15, 20 and 30-gallon charred oak barrels for aging. The smaller barrel has more wood in contact with the whiskey, causing it to age faster. Hot and cold temperature swings allow the barrel to expand and contract, imparting rich flavors to the whiskey.

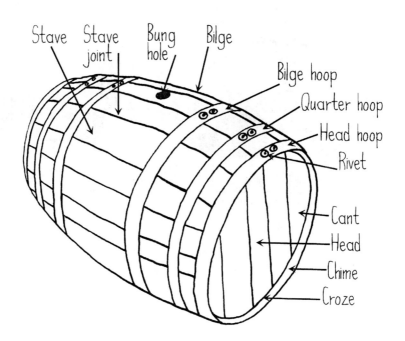

Stave Stave Bung Bilge
joint hole

Bilge hoop
Quarter hoop
Head hoop
Rivet
Cant
Head
Chime
Croze

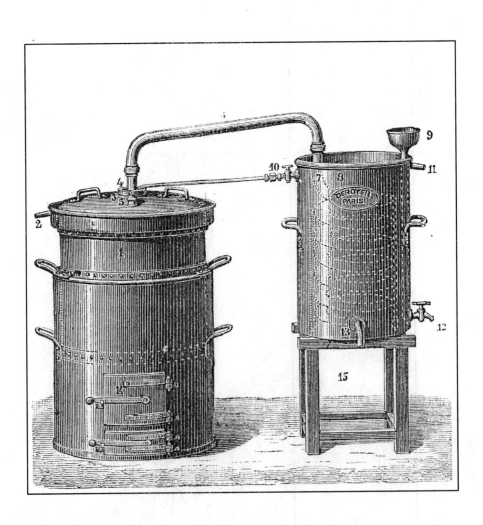

Q&A WHISKEY RECIPES

1. The difference between a Bourbon whiskey and a straight Bourbon whiskey is:

   [a] A straight Bourbon whiskey must have 100 percent of the base material, such as corn, whereas a Bourbon whiskey only has to have 51 percent.

   [b] A straight Bourbon whiskey has to be stored in a charred new American oak barrel for two years.

   [c] A straight Bourbon whiskey has to be stored in toasted new American oak barrels for two years.

2. In what way does the recipe between corn whiskey and Bourbon whiskey (either straight or regular Bourbon) differ?

   [a] A corn whiskey must be aged for a minimum of 3 years in new American oak barrels.

   [b] Bourbon, whether or not it is straight, must have at least 49 percent of the base material in the recipe, whereas a corn whiskey must have 100 percent.

   [c] A corn whiskey must be made from at least 80 percent corn, whereas Bourbon only needs to have 51 percent of the base material (corn).

3. Why might a modern artisan distiller choose to use smaller 15, 20, or 30-gallon charred oak barrels for aging his/her whiskey?

   [a] Because a smaller barrel allows the whiskey to have more surface contact with the wood, thus aging it faster.

   [b] Because smaller barrels are much cheaper than the standard 53 gallon barrels.

   [c] Because smaller barrels take up less space than the standard 53 gallon barrels.

4. The recipe for malt whiskey calls for:

   [a] 100 lbs. of 2-row barley malt and 20 lbs. of corn.

   [b] 61 lbs. of 2-row barley malt and 59 lbs. of rye.

   [c] 120 lbs. of 2-row barley malt.

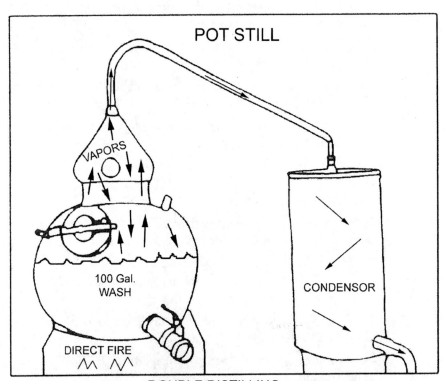

POT STILL

VAPORS

100 Gal.
WASH

CONDENSOR

DIRECT FIRE

DOUBLE DISTILLING

-Strippind 9% wash becomes 30% abv.
-Spirit run 30% abv becomes 70% abv. spirit
-Barrel aging

Chapter 10

How to Distill Whiskey (On a 100 gallon pot still)

Malt Whiskey

- Use 120-gallon fermentation tank
- Producing 100+ gallons of 9% abv wash

The Wash

- 275 lbs. 2-row barley malt
- Mashing time 45 minutes
- 30 oz. of yeast.
- Fermentation time 5- 7 days

[Important Note: When distilling malt whiskey it is very important to add the anti-foam agent Fermcap-S to the wash before distilling. This prevents the wash from foaming out of the still, and ending up in the parrot or collection pail.]

POT DISTILLATION OF MALT WHISKEY

Fill the still with 100 gallons of 9% abv wash. Most pot stills are direct-fired by propane, so heat the still slowly to avoid scorching the wash. It will take about 60 minutes to heat the wash to 173°F. At this temperature alcohol vapors start boiling off the wash and rise up and into the head of the still and into the condenser. Watch the head thermometer on the still and you will see it spike from 165° to 173°F as spirits "spit and sputter" as they come out of the condenser...*turn down the burner and...turn on the water to the condenser.* This action will slow the vapor buildup in the head of the still and the spitting and sputtering will stop. Toss this stuff. It will take another 15 minutes for the vapors to build back up and head temperature to reach 174°F. Again, the tube from the condenser will surge and spit a few times before becoming a small but steady stream running into a pail. *Collect and toss the first 4-6 ounces* before attaching the collection tube to the parrot with a hydrometer. For a quick reading use a density meter.

THE 100-GALLON RUN

Foreshots: At 174°F foreshots represent less than 2% of the distillate. Foreshots smell foul. Use them as a weed killer or to power your lawn mower.

Heads: At 175° to 190°F collect about 3 gallons. The abv will drop from 80 to 70%. Use a density meter or hydrometer and record the alcohol content, so you can duplicate the cuts at a later date. Use your nose and taste buds to assist in deciding where to cut your spirits.

Hearts: At 190° to 198°F collect 15 gallons. The abv will drop from 70 to 50% and average out to 65% abv (130 proof). Many whiskey distillers don't collect hearts below 50% abv.

Tails: At 200° to 205°F the abv will drop from 50% to 30%. Save these tails to be redistilled since tails contain congeners that give whiskey its classic flavor.

Note: At 30% abv a spoon full of spirits will fail to ignite. (Don't try this at home.) Below 30% toss everything.

DOUBLE DISTILLING

Ferment 8 bbls. or 240 gallons of 9% abv beer wash.

STRIPPING RUN

- 9% abv wash becomes 30% abv low wines.
- No cuts.
- Use Fermcap-S on all runs.
- Make three 80 gallon stripping runs. Each run will yield 27 gallons of low wines.
- The total amount collected, 81 gallons of 30% abv.
- To the 81 gallons add 19 gallons of water (Water extends the run allowing for better cuts).
- Now you are ready to double distill 100 gallons of low wine.

SPIRIT RUN

- 100 gallons of low wines, becomes 50 gallons of 70% spirit

The run

- Foreshots: The first 4-6 oz from the condenser contains aldehydes and other undesirable elements. Collect and use as a cleaning agent.
- Heads: Collect 10 gallons of 80 to 70 abv for re-distillation.
- Hearts: Collect 50 gallons of 70% to 50% abv for barreling.
- Tails: Collect 10 gallons 50% to 30% abv for redistilling. Toss anything below 30% abv.

There is a great deal of aroma and flavor in the tails fractions. Retaining a limited amount of the tails and then adding it back to the hearts adds complexity and depth. How much to include or when to stop collection tails for blending back is largely subjective (by taste) process that varies among distillers and their particular systems. You will need to experiment to determine what works best in your situation. Most important is keeping a record in a log book. Many distillers determine yields the old fashioned way, with an alcoholameter. If you decide to do so, find one with a range of 60 to 120, rather that using the widely available 0 to 200 models. The density meter gives faster results.

Note: At the end of the hearts run (50% abv) the alcohol coming out of the still is dropping and water is picked up as the boiling point goes higher, creating different flavors. Pot stills also often have temperature spikes in the head creating vapors with off-flavors of an anise or banana. It will take more than one distillation to learn how to control the flow of spirits from a pot still and collect the hearts from "the sweet spot."

AGING

- Age 6 months in a small, #4 char, new American oak barrel.
- Experiment with toasted applewood and cherrywood chips.
- Cut the spirits with distilled or reverse osmosis treated water.
- If using tap water to dilute, use a tight filter to remove sediment.

It is best to barrel age the whiskey in a building with no insulation. This allows summer and winter temperature variations to heat and cool the barrels ensuring a fast maturation. If possible, set a few barrel out in the sun for a couple of months. Barley, rye and wheat whiskies—unlike corn whiskey— don't require years of aging to pick up flavor and color from the barrel. Many believe that the flavor of corn whiskey comes from the barrel rather than the malt.

Many craft distillers own a German pot still with a tall column containing 5 to 25 plates. When distilling whiskey they make one pass hitting 65 abv, the spirits then go directly into the barrel. Some distillers run with the plates open and let the column create the reflux.

Many smaller distillers have a simple pot with no plates. Like the Scots, they double distill and on the second run collect 65% abv spirit for barreling.

Given your equipment and to see what work best, I suggest experimenting with single and double distillation runs. Remember, purists in the industry say double distilling produces a "richer" tasting product.

Q&A HOW TO DISTILL ON A 100 GALLON POT STILL

1. Before distilling malt whiskey, it is important to remember to add the Fermcap-S to the wash because:

    [a] Fermcap-S is an anti-foam agent which will prevent the distillate from foaming out of the still.

    [b] Fermcap-S will prevent the temperature inside the still from becoming too hot.

    [c] Fermcap-S adds some additional wild yeast to the wash, thus helping to produce desirable aromas which will carry over to the distillate.

2. During distillation, at 165°F, you should turn down the burner and turn on the water to the condenser because:

    [a] The still will explode if the temperature is allowed to keep rising.

    [b] This action will help to slow the buildup of vapors and will cool the distillate, and will stop the spitting and sputtering.

    [c] The water going into the condenser will create a reverse flow into the still, thus cooling down the wash.

3. During the production of a 100 gallon run, the foreshots represent what percentage of the distillate?

    [a] 60% of the distillate.

    [b] 2% of the distillate.

    [c] 20% of the distillate.

4. Between what temperatures, and between what abv, will you begin to collect 3 gallons of hearts?

    [a] The temperature will be between 190°F and 198°F degrees, and the abv will drop from 70 to 50%.

    [b] The temperature will be between 150°F to 174°F, and the abv will be 100% to 90%.

    [c] The temperature will be between 175°F to 190°F, and the abv will drop from 80% to 70%.

5. For any tails below 30% abv you should:

    [a] Toss.

    [b] Save and use it as a weed killer or fuel additive.

    [c] Redistill it, because all tails give whiskey their classic flavor.

6. The level of toasting required for your Bourbon whiskey barrels is:
  [a] A very light toast, # 1, so that you won't get any ash or charcoal in your whiskey.
  [b] No toasting or charring, because you want new, green wood that has not had any sort of fire in it.
  [c] A # 4 char in a new oak barrel, which is required by law and also gives your whiskey delicious vanilla and caramel flavors.

7. For a double distillation, the spirit run will yield:
  [a] 50 gallons of 70% abv spirit.
  [b] 10 gallons of 85% abv spirit.
  [c] 5 gallons of 30% abv spirit.

8. It is recommended that you age your whiskey in a building with:
  [a] Lots of insulation, so that the summer heat does not absorb all the water in the barrels.
  [b] No insulation, so that the summer and winter temperature variations heat and cool the barrels, thus aiding the maturation process.
  [c] A medium amount of insulation, so that the barrels won't get too cold in the winter.

Distilling Log

Date: _____

Volume of Wash: _____ abv: _____

Time: _____ Head Temperature: _____

ABV of First Cut (heads): _____ Volume: _____

Time to Run Hearts: _____ Minutes/140 to 90% abv

Hearts Volume: _____

Gravity of Tails: _____

Total Time / Start to Finish: _____

Volume of Hearts: _____

Notes: _____

_____

_____

_____

_____

_____

_____

_____

_____

_____

_____

_____

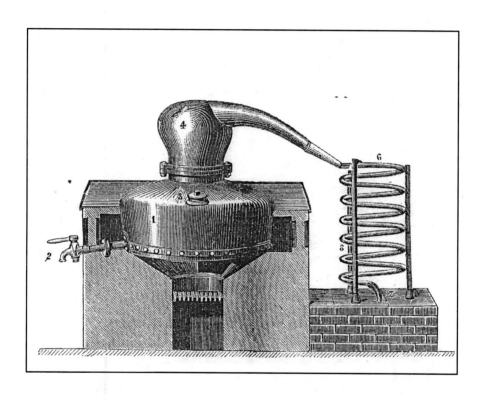

A Column Still

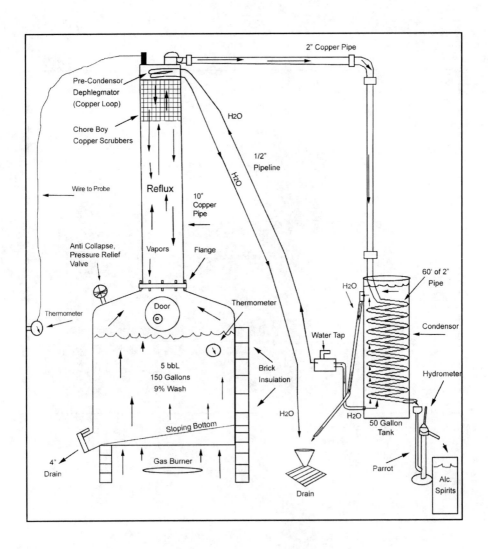

This is a best effort to illustrate a column still.

Chapter 11

Using a Simple Column Still

A pot distillation can increase the concentration of a 10% abv wort/wash to a 55% abv spirit. This first spirit is called low wines and before the second distillation it is diluted to 30% abv. This dilution will allow for accurate cuts during the second distillation by increasing the run time. After the 30% abv low wines are distilled, a 70-75% abv spirit is obtainable. In contrast, a pot still with a column with copper mesh packing and a dephlegmator (also known as a pre-condenser) can take the same 10% abv wash and on a single pass get a 60% abv or more spirit. Even more efficient is a column using trays and/or bubble caps.

Distilling in a single run produces a different whiskey than one produced by double distillation. This is because in double distillation, the dilution of the low wines with water before the second run allows better removal of negative congeners since there is more copper surface interaction and finer distillation control. This makes the spirit cleaner, less hot, and lighter tasting. The inclusion of a column with a pot still will additionally increase the ability of the distiller to control the congener content of the finished spirit with extreme precision.

The resulting products from each method (pot vs. column) have desirable qualities. It is up to the distiller to decide what process he or she wants to use and what style of whiskey to produce. The deciding factor may be in the price of the still. A 250-gallon pot still with a condenser runs about $150,000. A pot still with a column equipped with trays and bubble caps costs over $250,000. Non-professionally made stills can cost 1/10 this amount but require many engineering skills. A cheap 80-gallon pot still can be made for about $5,000, but this may be at the sake of performance and efficiency and therefore is rarely done for commercial use.

Many distillers, from Kentucky moonshiners to French cognac producers to German brandy makers, have developed their own unique still designs to improve the efficiency of a pot still. American moonshiners use a doubler, or a thumper keg. The French have a large helmet characteristic of the alambic still, and the Germans produce highly engineered stills with bubble plates.

While the equipment is different, the ultimate result of building a still that distills the spirit twice (or more) is one that all these pioneers were developing. To achieve a second distillation in a single run (using the column still), the vapor must condense briefly and then evaporate again. This process is easy to understand as traditional distillers accumulated their low wines so they would have a full still charge from which to perform a second distillation a few days later.

More complicated to understand, but identical in theory, is the construction of a still that automatically condenses, and then redistills, the spirit in a single run. American moonshiners used the thumper keg to do this. The thumper was placed between the still and the condenser, and was typically a pot 40 percent the size of the initial beer pot. The steam alcohol vapors from the still are injected into a tank with a water bath. Initially all of the vapors coming over from the still condense. As vapor subsequently continues to enter the thumper, the heat is transferred to the water bath/condensed vapor mixture. Finally the vapors will push their way through the bath when the temperature reaches more than 160ºF and they will flow into the condenser. The use of thumpers, however, is dangerous because pressure can build between the still and the thumper. This hazard can lead to explosion of the thumper tank and can also cause a still to implode. It is not recommended that any distillers use a pot still with a thumper. It will be rare that any commercial distillers will be allowed to operate a thumper equipped still due to the lack of ASME-rated safety devices. Instead, most artisan distillers have a pot still with four or five plates in the column. The column pot still typically has plates equipped with bubble cups and a deflegmator. This type of still is readily available. Some of the best whiskey in the world is produced using a simple pot still with a condenser, but if you can invest in equipment that allows for better efficiency and effectiveness it can reduce the production and aging time of the whiskey. An ideal system would be one comprised of a pot still with a 4-plate column, deflegmator, and a condenser.

THE COLUMN DISTILLATION PROCESS

At 173°F, vapors from the wash begin to rise up the column and hit the copper mesh packing or plates in the column. At the top of the column is a jacket or heat exchanger (deplegmator/pre-condenser) through which cool water is circulated. The combination of the surface area of the packing and the cool water heat exchange causes the rising vapors to cool. The condensed vapor then cascades down the column and through the packing or trays allowing it to fall back into the wash where it is re-heated. This process is called reflux distillation. Some systems use the warmed water exiting the condenser to cool the dephlegmator/pre-condenser. Although this can save some water, by using colder water and slowing down the flow exiting the dephlegmator/pre-condenser, finer control of the purity of the spirit can be achieved.

Soon reflux will push past the packing or trays and the dephlegmator/pre-condenser and the system will be in balance. At this point the alcohol vapors from the wash will have lined themselves up by their atomic weight with the lightest vapors (heads) coming off first followed by the hearts and tails.

A typical whiskey second distillation run on a packed or plate column still should be controlled to start running off between 80% and 75% abv and stopped between 64% abv to 64.9% abv.

During the distilling process the distiller must be very careful not to over-cool the dephlegmator/pre-condenser. Doing so with a non-safety equipped system will cause the alcohol to condense quickly and possibly collapse the still. All distilling systems should be equipped with a pressure and vacuum safety valve. In a safety-equipped system, over-cooling of the dephelgmator/pre-condenser will only result in stopping the flow of spirit from the condenser and will avoid disastrous results.

The distiller can control the percent of alcohol of the spirit by increasing or decreasing the heat to the pot. If your distillation system includes a dephlegmator/pre-condenser, the control is achieved by increasing or decreasing the amount of water running through it.

Increasing reflux = higher proof and purity, slower run. Decreasing reflux = lower proof and purity, faster run.

Clean sweet spirits can be obtained by running a "cold still." This is accomplished by keeping the head temperature of the still under 180°F. This is done by running a significant amount of water through the dephlegmator/pre-condenser cooling the top portion of the column which will increase condensation and thereby allowing greater reflux.

The head fraction collected on an average whiskey run will be about 21% of the total alcohol. Hearts will be about 57%. The tails will be about 22%. Whiskey distillers re-distill the tails because they contain very concentrated flavorful congeners, but typically discard the head fraction.

The still must be cleaned after every use by flushing it with hot water, and weekly by cleaning it with 2% caustic (sodium hydroxide) followed by a 2% citric acid wash.

CONCLUSION

Every distillery is different. Each decision, shape, style and size affects the final product. The goal should be to produce a whiskey that is consistently reproducible from batch to batch as efficiently as your system will allow.

Q&A HOW TO DISTILL USING A TRADITIONAL POT AND COLUMN STILL

1. Before running a second distillation on a pot still, it is advisable to dilute your low wine with water to 30% abv because:

   [a] A simple pot still is too primitive to distill low wines as high as 55% abv.

   [b] The dilution will increase the run time so that more accurate cuts can be made.

   [c] The law insists upon it.

2. One of the differences in the whiskey produced by double distillation versus distilling in a single run is:

   [a] By using double distillation, the spirit is cleaner and lighter tasting since negative congeners are removed by the increased copper contact.

   [b] There really is no difference in the whiskeys produced by both methods.

   [c] By using single distillation, the spirit is cleaner and lighter tasting than the whiskey made by double distillation because more negative congeners are removed.

3. A pot still with a column with copper mesh packing and a dephlegmator can take a 10 percent wash and on a single pass get 70 to 75% abv spirit, while distilling a 30 percent low wine distilled on a pot still will only obtain a 60% abv spirit.

   [a] True

   [b] False

4. What was the main problem with the "thumper," or doubler, used by traditional Kentucky moonshiners?

   [a] The thumper was too expensive for the average moonshiner to buy.

   [b] The large helmet or onion shape characteristic of the thumper was inefficient.

   [c] Pressure would frequently build up between the thumper and the still, causing dangerous explosions.

5. The process known as "reflux" refers to:

    [a] The product is distilled twice, allowing distillers to increase the strength and quality of their whiskey.

    [b] A serious gastroesophageal disease common among distillers, caused by excessive sampling of the new spirits while making the cuts.

    [c] A still design that allows the distiller to increase the strength and quality of whiskey in a single run by allowing the vapors to briefly condense, be reheated, and then evaporate again.

6. Because of the danger of over-cooling the dephlegmator/pre-condenser, whereby the alcohol quickly condenses and the still could possibly collapse all distilling systems should be equipped with:

    [a] An alarm that sounds when the dephlegmator gets over-cooled.

    [b] A pressure and vacuum safety valve.

    [c] The system should have the dephlegmator taken off, since the design is inherently dangerous.

7. Increasing the reflux = higher proof and purity, and a slower run, while decreasing reflux = lower proof and purity, faster run.

    [a] True

    [b] False

8. Running a "cold still" by keeping the head temperature of the still under 180°F:

    [a] Produces a foul-tasting spirit.

    [b] Does not produce anything, because the still needs heat to distill the product.

    [c] Produces a very clean, sweet spirit.

9. On the average whiskey run, the fractions will more or less be as thus:

    [a] Heads fraction 57%; hearts fraction 22%; and tails fraction 21%.

    [b] Heads fraction 21%; hearts fraction 57%; and tails fraction 22%.

    [c] Heads fraction 3%; hearts fraction 45%; and tails fraction 52%.

Appendices

Appendix A

The Spread Sheet for Small Distillery

Craig Pakish is the owner of C&C Shine, a moonshine distiller is located in Gonzalez, CA. Craig was kind enough to share the costs to open C&C. He said "Every corner was cut to get into the business."

Spread Sheet for C&C Shine

My Month One:

Form LLC, Attorney Fees:	$3,000

Month Two:

Apply for use permit through City of Gonzales

• Fees:	$2,000
• Building Rent:	$720.00
• ABC TTB Consultant:	$800.00
• ABC License, 3 each, fee:	$800
	(Federal License Fee)

Month Three Through Ten:

• Rent:	$7,200

• Retrofit Building

    Building fire walls
    Building Handicap Bathroom
    Pave and paint handicap parking and fire lanes

Build fire sprinkler system	$65,240

Contract plumbing and electrical

NOX Box for fire department	$50
Total costs including building permits, labor, material	*$79,810*

Month Ten:

• Trademarks and business Licenses:	$380
• Equipment: Still,	$3,200

Used barrels for mashing, free.

Stainless steel dairy tanks,	$6,400

(Turned out they were useless—
Lesson Learned: hire a consultant before buying tanks).

Bottle Filler & Labeler:	$2,000

Month Eleven:

• Label design:	$60/ hour.
• COLA fee	
• Label tooling and printing:	$3,000

[$0.85 each (2,160 bottles) plus shipping from Texas]

• Bottles: $2,160	
• Hydrometer, Thermometers	$351
• Office equipment: Phone/fax, phone lines	$300

Month Twelve:

• Purchase yeast, grain and sugar	$1,000
• Water system for production and cleaning (ozone water)	$8,000
• Forklift, borrow as needed from neighboring business.	
• Racks for storage, free	
• Misc. pumps, hoses and fittings	$2,000

Grand Total	***$108,601***
	estimated

Appendix B
The Code of Federal Regulations

www.ttb.gov/spirits/chapter4.pdf

1. "Whiskey" is an alcoholic distillate from a fermented mash of grain produced at less than 190° proof in such manner that the distillate possesses the taste, aroma, and characteristics generally attributed to whiskey, stored in oak containers (except that corn whiskey need not be so stored), and bottled at not less than 80° proof, and also includes mixtures of such distillates for which no specific standards of identity are prescribed.

a. "Bourbon whiskey," "rye whiskey," "wheat whiskey," "malt whiskey," or "rye malt whiskey" is whiskey produced at not exceeding 160° proof from a fermented mash of not less than 51 percent corn, rye, wheat, malted barley, or malted rye grain, respectively, and stored at not more than 125° proof in charred new oak containers; and also includes mixtures of such whiskeys of the same type.

b. "Corn whiskey" is whiskey produced at not exceeding 160° proof from a fermented mash of not less than 80 percent corn grain, and if stored in oak containers stored at not more than 125° proof in used or uncharred new oak containers and not subjected in any manner to treatment with charred wood; and also includes mixtures of such whiskey.

The above whiskeys which have been stored in the type of oak containers noted, for a period of 2 years or more can be designated as "straight;" for example, "straight Bourbon whiskey," "straight corn whiskey." However, if produced from a fermented mash of less than 51 percent of any one type of grain, and stored for a period of 2 years or more in charred new oak containers its proper designation is merely "straight whiskey." No other whiskeys may be designated "straight." Additionally, "straight whiskey" can include mixtures of straight whiskeys of the same type produced in the same State.

"Whiskey distilled from Bourbon (rye, wheat, malt, or rye malt) mash" is whiskey produced in the United States at not exceeding 160° proof from a fermented mash of not less than 51 percent corn, rye, wheat, malted barley, or malted rye grain, respectively, and stored in used oak containers; and also includes mixtures of such whiskeys of the same type. However, Whiskey conforming to the standard of identity for corn whiskey must be designated corn whiskey.

"Light whiskey" is whiskey produced in the United States at more than 160° proof, on or after January 26, 1968, and stored in used or un-charred new oak containers; and also includes mixtures of such whiskeys. If "light whiskey" is mixed with less than 20 percent of straight whiskey on a proof gallon basis, the mixture shall be designated "blended light whiskey" (light whiskey—a blend).

"Blended whiskey" (whiskey—a blend) is a mixture which contains straight whiskey or a blend of straight whiskeys at not less than 20 percent on a proof gallon basis, excluding alcohol derived from added harmless coloring, flavoring or blending materials, and, separately, or in combination, whiskey or neutral spirits. A blended whiskey containing not less than 51 percent on a proof gallon basis of one of the types of straight whiskey shall be further designated by that specific type of straight whiskey; for example, "blended rye whiskey" (rye whiskey—a blend).

"A blend of straight whiskeys" (blended straight whiskeys) is a mixture of straight whiskeys which does not conform to the standard of identify for "straight whiskey." Products so designated may contain harmless coloring, flavoring, or blending materials as allowable by regulations.

"A blend of straight whiskeys" (blended straight whiskeys) consisting entirely of one of the types of straight whiskey, and not conforming to the standard for straight whiskey, shall be further designated by that specific type of straight whiskey; for example, "a blend of straight rye whiskeys" (blended straight rye whiskeys). "A blend of straight whiskeys" consisting entirely of one of the types of straight whiskey shall include straight whiskey of the same type which was produced in the same State or by the same proprietor within the same State, provided that such whiskey contains harmless coloring, flavoring, or blending materials as allowable by law.

Neutral spirits or alcohol may only appear in a "blend of straight whiskeys" or in a "blend of straight whiskeys consisting entirely of one of the types of straight whiskey" as a vehicle for recognized flavoring of blending material.

c. "Spirit whiskey" is a mixture of neutral spirits and not less than 5 percent on a proof gallon basis of whiskey, or straight whiskey, or straight whiskey and whiskey, if the straight whiskey component is less than 20 percent on a proof gallon basis.

Appendix C
Grand Application
Farm Distiller

Many farmers have a surplus of fruit; distilling is another potential marketplace for their crops. This is called "value added" as they are adding value to existing resources, (i.e. fruit that is going to waste or sold at a market price making growing it unprofitable).

To obtain money for a feasibly study a farmer can apply to his/her state's department of agriculture for financial support.

Thanks to Jim Pierce for sharing this grant proposal.

APPLICATION FORMAT

I. APPLICANT INFORMATION:
Project Name(s): Apple Eaux de Vie (Brandy) Distillery
Contact person: Jim Pierce
Address: 38215 W. 176th Street
City, State, Zip: Rayville MO 64084
Phone: 660.232.1096
Fax: na
Email: piercejim@hotmail.com
Cost of Project: $ 60,500
Grant Application Amount: $ 55,000

II. PROJECT SUMMARY
Missouri fruit prices are pressured down by the improvement of orchard techniques, foreign imports, interstate imports, limited window of opportunity for fresh consumption, and the slow process of changeover to new varieties.

Paralleling this is the growing trend for consuming local, not only food but products. There is also a trend of increasing spirit consumption and interests in locally distilled products. Federal and state laws have changed to allow for micro-distilling as well.

There appears to be the opportunity to match excessive and low priced fruit with consumption of locally distilled spirits. New uses would put price pressure on the raw material, in this case, apples, helping increase gross revenue for fruit growers.

We would like to contract a marketing firm to help assess and quantify the need of producers for new products based on their crop, the market size for fruit brandies, the potential value added by distilling, and the economic benefits of a micro-distillery based in Ray County.

With positive data and a business plan in hand, we expect to begin the next step of beginning the development of a distillation branch producing Eau de Vie at Of The Earth in Ray County for regional sales.

III. IDENTIFICATION OF NEED

Low apple prices are a problem. Apple prices in the state of Missouri are currently depressed (1,4).Orchard numbers are shrinking (6).Influx of imported fruit and the glut of seasonal production of fruit provide down pressure. The market for fresh local consumption is a narrow window and by its nature limited.

An alternative use for local surplus is needed. With national trends of Eat Local, consume local and increases in spirit consumption, the opportunity exists for locally produced value-added products for consumers and a void exists for a locally produced premium 100 percent fruit brandy, Eau de Vie.

There is an increasing national trend of micro-distilling in the nation (3). Spirit consumption has risen every year the last 9 years (2,5). There are 2 micro-distillers operating in the state of Missouri: Augusta, St. Louis, and 1 near beginning operation at Branson. Nationally there were 40 licensed makers in 2003 which grew to more than 150 in 2008 and many more in the pipeline. (3) By adding value to our apples, as source material, distilling an eau de vie we could provide added income directly to our orchard and locally push wholesale apple prices up. New uses for price-depressed apples will help fruit producers with increased prices by putting pressure on base prices for the state, and distilling adds jobs in manufacturing, construction, and sales. The distillery/orchard, as a destination, will also provide indirect economic development potential for the rural community creating jobs for associated day trip activities, "staycations." The micro-distillery will provide an example for other producers in the state.

IV. STATEMENT OF OBJECTIVES

We would like to discover the increase in spirit consumption, and the size of the market not currently being met for local, craft distilled product. The new wave of micro-distilling could provide rural jobs directly, tourism and support industries jobs indirectly and a new market for Missouri apples for Bates, Clay, Caldwell, Carroll, Chariton, Lafayette, and Ray counties. Bates, Chariton and Lafayette are the 3 largest orchard acres in the state and all counties are located in the central western part of the state surrounding Kansas City.

It is already proven to be technically feasible (7,8),with over 150 registered micro-distillers nationally, 2 in Missouri.

Is regional distillation of apples to a eau de vie-style brandy potentially profitable, to what extent, and, if it is, what is the path to implementing?

Phase 1

>   Feasibility study of the market situation

>   Raw material sources

>   Need for new use—Midwest Fruit grower survey

>   Market demand for 100 percent fruit brandies

>   Consumer profile

>   Economic feasibility

>   Profit potential

>   Measure growth potential

>   Focus groups

>   Regional economic impact

Phase 2

>   Business plan

>   SWOT

>   Market plan

>   Production plan

>   Finance plan

Phase 3

>   Implementation

>   Presenting the plan to the bank

>   Presenting the plan to investors

This will affect Ray County, directly with the establishment of a local distillery and indirectly the surrounding counties. There exists the possibility of lifting local apple prices as demand for fruit increases with additional production and new micro-distillers. With a greater profit potential in fruit production, new acreage may be added increasing farm incomes and creating opportunity for new farms and associated industries. Several jobs in the processing of apples into product will be created. Jobs in sales, distribution, research and development will occur. Not to mention the potential to develop state highway I-210 the distiller's row extending into Carroll County. As a tourist destination these distilleries, located close to source orchards, would encourage associated restaurants, shops, fuel stops to follow. Byproduct uses such as compost, flavorings for grilling, and dried horse "chips" are possible from mash after extracting.

V. EXPECTED RESULTS AND APPLICABILITY TO DEVELOPMENT

Expect to verify markets for craft distilled brandies do exist and define them. Use the market research and capital sources to write a business plan for Of The Earth to use in beginning eau de vie production, creating a tourist destination, from our own apple production and expansion through purchasing of apples from surrounding counties to service these markets. The market is expected to be far greater than the production of one craft distiller so that similar enterprises can also help create jobs in rural Missouri, making contributions to the local economy and state treasury through taxes.

Technical merit— Artisan distilling: 40 licensed makers in 2003 to more than 150 in 2008 (1-ADI)

Distilling currently being taught at Southwest Missouri State, Springfield and Michigan State University. At least 2 micro-distilleries operating in MO now.

Project specific qualifications of principals, subs: James D Pierce: BS in Horticulture at NWMS, 15 years growing fruits and vegetables, several years of home juice/wine production, 1 year of juice production for market.

Potential for direct near-term commercial application of project's results:

According to the ADI forum, startup times are ranging from to 2-3 years. Our hope is that information gathered will allow immediate application for funds and production/marketing to begin as soon as capital acquired.

Anticipated results: New product development for fruit and use of locally produced commodity to satisfy a market trend creating new jobs and through competitive uses for apples push base price up and providing security to existing orchards. A profitable product for Of The Earth.

Impact on MO ag producers: Increase demand for MO fruit mid- to long-term.

Impact on rural community economy: The states of Washington, Oregon, and Michigan have fledgling micro distillery industries. Michigan expects a 400 million dollar contribution to its state economy. We expect to bring in new jobs distilling, sales of value added product, and associated development. Send capital to surrounding counties producing apples, increase county tax income, and the possibility of beginning a distilling "trail" along I-210, linking locally produced ag products, value added products and associated increase in service, restaurants, fuel.

Job creation potential: Michigan's expectations were a $400 million contribution to their state economy as a result of law changes allowing microdistillation.

Of The Earth expects to create near-term 1-4 construction jobs, after production starts 1-2 in distilling and sales. The market and our research will then determine growth for Of The Earth. Countywide or even statewide replication of regional distilling businesses based on our findings could establish a state industry with results paralleling Michigan.

Capital investment:

Loader, bulk bins for harvest

Cost of building-restrooms, warehouse, production, office, sign.

Equipment—sink, 2 ton flatbed truck, tank wash, pallet jack, fruit mill, pulp pump, fermentation vessels, mash pump, reflux still, holding tank, pulp disposal bins, bottle filler, labeler, pallets, cleaning equipment.

Office furnishings—computer, business software, desk, file cabinet.

Tasting room—counter, register, display shelves, glasses, sink, signage.

Actual costs are expected to come from preparing Business Plan with grant findings.

PLAN OF WORK

Key personnel
Patricia Pierce, James C. Pierce, and James D. Pierce

Consultants
EEMG, Kansas City, MO

Bill Owens—industry contact

Financial—Westbrook and Associates

Equipment Manufacturer contacted—Bavarian Breweries and Distilleries

Kris Berglund, Michigan State University

Week 1-8 (8 weeks)
Begin Phase 1, Feasibility study.

Begin interviewing operating micro distilleries and education research facilities about startup costs, equipment costs, cost of production.

Week 9-13 (4 weeks)
Phase 2: build the business plan.

Week 14-17 (3 weeks)
Phase 3: Implement.

II. FACILITIES AND EQUIPMENT
Existing office, computer, and phone owned by Of The Earth.

VIII. CO-SPONSORS
None yet.

IX. REFERENCES
Bill Owens
Kris Berglund

1) Marilyn Odneal, SWMS, phone conversation 9/23/08.

2) http://articles.moneycentral.msn.com/Investing/Extra/BourbonBusinessBooms.aspx?GT1=33002

3) American Distilling Institute

4) Paul Peters, conversation 9/17/2008

5) Article, http://www.drinksmediawire.com/afficher_cdp.
asp?id=1681&lng=2 <http://www.drinksmediawire.com/afficher_cdp.
asp?id=1681&lng=2>

6) MO orchard statistics
http://www.nass.usda.gov/census/census02/volume1/mo/
st29_2_030_030.pdf

7) ADI #92, Apples into Vodka

8) ADI#, Atchison Distiller, grains into whiskey

Literature Search

1) Article, MI state law change, expect 400 million economic impact http://
news.msu.edu/story/5614

Of The Earth presently sells apples for fresh consumption at 1 local retail location and 1 local farmer's market. Production comes from 265 apple trees, 15 varieties, that are in their 13th year. There are 300 more apple trees of various ages planted but not of bearing age. The farm sits on 3 parcels, 2 sited next to each other comprising 40 acres of which 20 acres of pasture that could be planted to orchard. The 3rd parcel is a retail location where our greenhouse is built along a main highway, I-210, a main thoroughfare to Kansas City, placing it 30 minutes from downtown Kansas City.

Current orchard production is sold fresh with approximately 14 percent of total crop marketed through the Liberty Farmer's market, Lawson Farmer's market, and at the greenhouse. Some culls are converted to juice. Fresh prices average 50 cents per pound, $21 per bushel. Juice sells for $10 a gallon. A bushel yields 2 gallons, so, it takes 21.5 pounds of fruit, which nets 46.5 cents per pound. We lose 3.5 cents a pound by making juice.

We're selling 14 percent of the current fruit off producing trees, 185 bushel. Several varieties have turned out to not be suited to our environment for the fresh market but would make juice. The confluence of limits of our own labor, excess production, and the local fresh market demand are balanced.

There is less than 6 acres planted with potentially 25 acres to expand into but with prices at 2.52 for processors at wholesale it makes the wholesale market consideration moot.

Our apple production, limited as it is, has outstripped our 3 marketing venues. Therefore, regional varietal eau de vie production could add value and raise our gross revenues. Development of the equipment combined with the orchard and eau de vie production as a tourist attraction will also increase income for the business. Regional varietal brandies open the door to many locally small distilleries across the state. Creating jobs in operation, repair/maintenance, marketing, orchards, and tourism.

Small Distillery Startup

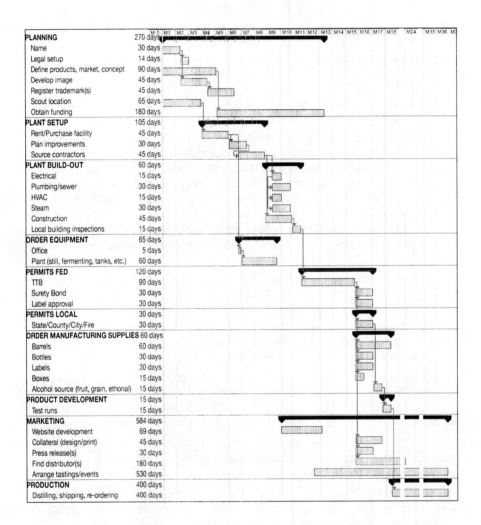

PLANNING	270 days
Name	30 days
Legal setup	14 days
Define products, market, concept	90 days
Develop image	45 days
Register trademark(s)	45 days
Scout location	65 days
Obtain funding	180 days
PLANT SETUP	105 days
Rent/Purchase facility	45 days
Plan improvements	30 days
Source contractors	45 days
PLANT BUILD-OUT	60 days
Electrical	15 days
Plumbing/sewer	30 days
HVAC	15 days
Steam	30 days
Construction	45 days
Local building inspections	15 days
ORDER EQUIPMENT	65 days
Office	5 days
Plant (still, fermenting, tanks, etc.)	60 days
PERMITS FED	120 days
TTB	90 days
Surety Bond	30 days
Label approval	30 days
PERMITS LOCAL	30 days
State/County/City/Fire	30 days
ORDER MANUFACTURING SUPPLIES	60 days
Barrels	60 days
Bottles	30 days
Labels	30 days
Boxes	15 days
Alcohol source (fruit, grain, ethonal)	15 days
PRODUCT DEVELOPMENT	15 days
Test runs	15 days
MARKETING	584 days
Website development	69 days
Collateral (design/print)	45 days
Press release(s)	30 days
Find distributor(s)	180 days
Arrange tastings/events	530 days
PRODUCTION	400 days
Distilling, shipping, re-ordering	400 days

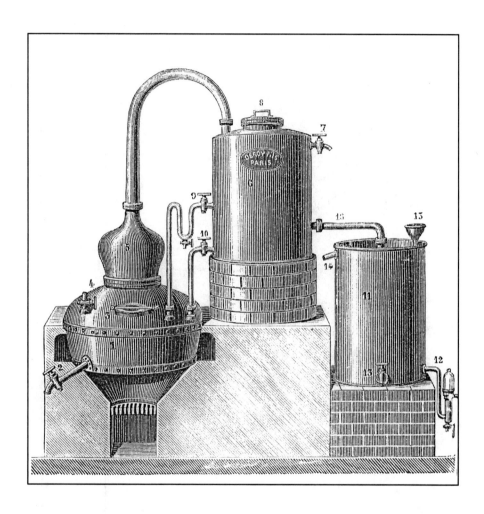

Appendix D
Moonshine Vocabulary

Alley Alley Bourbon.

Autumn Leaf Makes your face change color and you fall to the ground.

Balm of Gilead Moonshine slang.

Blue John Moonshine slang.

Bottled in Barn Play on the expression "bottled in bond."

Brannigan Brandy, Buckeye Bark Whiskey

Bumblings Noise created in the drinker's head Bush Whiskey, Canned Heat, Cannonball Swig, Chain Lighting, Chicago Joy Juice: Are terms for moonshine.

Chicken Whiskey Two drinks and you don't care where you lay.

City Gin Moonshine

Coffee County Rye Giving big shots "local moonshine" and calling it county rye.

Coffee Varnish, Cool Water, Corn Squeezin's. Moonshine terms.

Creepin' Whiskey Creeps up behind you and knocks you to your knees.

Dead Man's Dram So strong that if you can make and unconscious person swallow some he or she will remember it when coming to

Deep Shaft Kansas Moonshine.

Embalming Fluid "Gut rot."

Forty-rod How far you are from reality before you pass out. Or, the distance it make you run before you pass out.

Happy Sally, Jump Steady. Moonshine terms.

Monkey Rum Moonshine from the "sand hills" region of North and South Carolina. Made from molasses.

Moon, Mooney The beveage of choice, made from molasses in, Pittsburgh, PA. during prohibition. Described as "malodorous fir water" costing $2 a gallon. Mountain Dew, Old Horsey, Panther's Breath, Panther's Pizen, Pine Top, Pop Skull, Preacher's Lye, Radiator Whiskey, Red Eye, Roasing-ear-wine.

Rot Gut Adulterated liquor.

Ruckus Juice, Scorpion Juice. Moonshine slang.

Seven Stars A moonshiner's exclamation.

Shinny, Skull Cracker. Moonshine slang

Soda Pop Moon Bottled in a soda bottle.

Splo The explosion it causes in your gut.

Squirrel Whiskey, Stingo, Strike Me Dead. Stump Whiskey, Stumphole, Sump puller.

Sugar Whiskey Whiskey made from sugar. Swam Root, Sweet Spirits of Cats a Fighting, Tiger Spit, Tiger's Sweat.

White Mule "White" because it is clear, "mule" because of the kick.

Who Shot John Produces instant unconsciousness.

Wildcat.

These synonyms from the book *Moonshiners, Bootleggers and Rumrunners.*

Appendix E

Information about TTB and Licensing a Distillery

DSP DISTILLING SPIRITS PLANTS

The Tobacco Tax and Trade Bureau (TTB) lists over 350 Distilling Spirits Plants (DSP) "license distilleries" of which 165 are craft distilleries. The rest of the companies are whiskey distilleries, industrial distillers, rectifiers, and importers. If you want to know anything about a distilling company, search for company information online. Many marketing companies who sell lots of whiskey claim to be a "distillery company" but other companies distill and bottle for them.

Support your local distillery and buy products that say "hand-crafted." Join the American Distilling Institute, (www.distilling.com), and support its efforts to education the public about the art and science of distilling.

TO START THE LICENSING PROCESS FOR A DISTILLERY GO TO:

- Distilled spirits permits http://www.ttb.gov/spirits/index.shtml
- Distilled Spirits Laws and Regulations http://www.ttb.gov/spirits spirits_regs.shtml
- CFR's "styles of whiskey" http://www.ttb.gov/spirits/chapter4.pdf
- TTB statistics on distilling go to: www.ttb.gov then to "spirits" and then the "year."
- State Alcohol Boards:
  http://www.ttb.gov/wine/control_board.shtml
- Material Safety Data Sheet (http://en.wikipedia.org/wiki).

Appendix F
Resources

CATALOGS & SUPPLIES

AceHardware.com	Stainless steel cooler on wheels
Artisan-distiller.net	Information and distilling supplies
Amphora-Society.com	Small distillery & distilling supplies
Crosby-baker.com	Full line of ingredients, supplies for breweries & wineries
GWKent.com	Brewing, winemaking distilling supplies
Prosperoequipment.com	Wine, brewing & distilling equipment supplies
TCW-Web.com	Equipment for wine and spirits
Americanmercantile.net	Importer of spices
Grainger.com	Thousands of items for a distillery or brewery

DISTILLING EQUIPMENT MANUFACTURERS

[Note: Equipment companies do not have time or the resources to explain the distillation process to beginners. Educate yourself before contacting them.]

Vendome Copper & Brass Works	**vendome.com** 502-587-1930
Forsyth	**forsyth.com** +44-1340-831-787
Kothe Distilling Technologies	**kothe-distilling.com** 571-278-1313
Bavarian-Holstein Partners	**potstills.com** 310-391-1091
CARL Distilleries	**brewing-distilling.com** 215-242-6806
Adrian Edelbrande GmbH	**koenigdistillery.com** 208-455-8386
Chalvignac Prulho Distillation	**groupe-novtech.com** +133-6-22-15-22-15
Mueller Brennereianlagen	**foothillrocks@deiter.ca** 250-503-4731

ALAMBIC AND MOONSHINE STILLS

10 to 300 gallon stills

Copper Moonshine Stills	coppermoonshinestills.com 479-414-3220
Hoga Company	hogacompany.com 351 226 062430
Iberian Coppers S.A.	copper-alembic.com 351 251 823370
Oregon Copper Works	oregoncopperbowl.com 541-485-9845
Revenoor	revenoor.com 503-662-4173
Dynamic Alambic	dynamicalambic.com 509-398-3321
Amphora-Society	amphora-society.com 206-527-5520

SUPPLIERS OF EQUIPMENT AND INGREDIENTS

1. www.**Brewhaus**.com
2. www.**Morebeer**.com
3. www.**Northernbrewer**.com
4. www.**Williamsbrewing**.com
5. www.**Oakbarrel**.com
6. www.**Greatfermentations**.com
7. www.**Breworganic**.com
8. www.**Bwmwct**.com
9. www.**Beernut**.com
10. www.**Maltos**.com
11. www.**home-distilling**.com
12. www.fermentationbiz.com
13. www.promash.com

Complete list of suppliers at www.beertown.org

Recommended Reading

TECHNICAL DISTILLING BOOKS

1. *Whiskey: Technology, Production and Marketing* edited by Inge Russell, Charles Bamforth, and Graham Stewart. ISBN 9780126692020.

2. *Fermented Beverage Production*, second edition (paperback) by Andrew G.H. Lea (Editor) and John R. Piggott (Editor).

3. *Fundametals of Distillery Practice* by Herman F. Willkie and Joseph A. Prochaska; published by Joseph E. Seagram & Sons; 1943.

4. *The Science and Technology of Whiskeys* edited by J. R. Piggott, R. E. Duncan, & R. Sharp ISBN 9780582044289

5. *Distilled Beverage Flavour* edited by J.R. Piggott and A. Patterson; Ellis Horwood Series in Food Science and Technology. (This isn't for beginners).

6. *The Alcohol Textbook* is sold out. Order the CD http://www.murtagh.com/textbook-4-CD.html

7. *The Whiskey Distilleries of the United Kingdom* by Alfred Barnard; 1887. This was reprinted in 1969 and again more recently.

8. *The Manufacture of Whiskey and Plain Spirit* by J.A. Nettleton; 1913. And his 8 other books published from 1881 to 1897.

BOOKS FOR THE START UP DISTILLER

1. *Making Pure Corn Whiskey* by Ian Smiley; www.home-distilling.com

2. *The Complete Distiller* by Mike McCaw; www.amphora-society.com

3. *Alcohol Distilleŕs Handbook* Desert Publications; info@deltapress.com

4. *Distillers Manual* White Mule Press; available from www.distilling.com

5. *Practical Distiller* by Samual McHarry; www.raudins.com/brewbooks

6. *Cider*, a Story Publishing Book; 800-793-9396

7. *Whiskey* by Michael Jackson; ISBN 0-7894-9710-7; www.dk.com

8. *Moonshine Made Simple* by Byron Ford; byronfordbooks@hotmail.com

9. *Moonshine* by Matthew Rowley; ISBN 978-1-57990-648-1 (Amazon)

10. *Craft Whiskey Distilling* www.distilling.com

11. *How to Build A Small Brewery* www.distilling.com

12. *Alcohol Distillers Manual for Gasohol and Spirits* (Quality Books)

Appendix G

No Yeast Necessary

(from the internet)

We used 55-gallon barrels or 53-gallon oak whiskey barrels. Take 100 lb. of cracked yellow corn. (This corn needs to be air dried, not dried by gas, since gas drying takes the goodies out of it). Put the corn meal in the barrel, and then put about 40 gallons of good water in your cooker and heat the water to about 100°F degrees. Drain the water by the bucketfull and stir your sugar in so it is well dissolved. We used 50 lbs., or sometimes 60 lbs. of sugar on the first barrel.

Here's probably what is different, we DID NOT add any YEAST of any kind to this. If the temperature is in the mid 90°Fs this would work off in 5 to 7 days. About day 2 or 3 it sounded like Rice Krispies that just had milk poured over them. Again, no yeast was added. We did take a wood paddle and stirred it once or twice a day. In the old days, all there was available was baker's yeast, and adding baker's yeast caused an off taste, hiccups, indigestion or heartburn, so that is why it was left out. In cold weather sometimes yeast was used to get the first barrel going.

When the mash got "dog heads" on it, that's when the large single bubbles come about 20-30 seconds apart. It was ready to cook off. The mash also had a sour taste to it. On a 50 or so gallon cooker with two propane burners, shine would start running in about an hour. The cooling barrel was also about 55 gallon with a ⅝" inch by 40' copper worm, which had cold water running in the top and discharging water coming out mid ways. Most of the time the discharging water came at the bottom of the barrel. This first run would usually start at about 120-125 proof and would run down to about 80 proof. This was strained through a heavy white felt hat, and sometimes a double handful of hickory charcoal was also used in the hat. This 80-125 proof would be put to the side to keep, but the still kept running from the 80 proof on down to about 45-50 proof, this would be about a gallon and we called it singles. The 80-125 proof would be about 4 gallons.

Cut off the cooker when it is somewhere between 45-50 proof and the beer cools down to about 100°F. Take about three, 3lb. coffee cans of your meal out of the barrel and put the same amount of fresh meal back in (this makes a difference in your next yield and proof), then mix another 60 lbs.

of sugar to your warm beer and put back in your mash barrel and stir it. Then let it work off again.

On your second run, put your beer in the cooker and also the gallon of singles you saved out. This run here should start out about 135 proof, having seen it go to 140. After a gallon or so it may be 120 and stay 120 for an hour or better before it drops lower in proof. This run usually lasts about 2 ½-3 hours and makes about 9 gallons. Again, quit saving it when it gets to 80 proof but keep running till it is down to the 45-50 proof for your singles. It will make about 2 gallons or so this run, repeat the whole process 2 times or more. Don't forget to take some old meal out and put same amount of fresh back in each time and also pour the singles back in the cooker. I don't think I've ever seen the proof get above 140, but have seen 11-gallon yields.

On your very last cooking, pour all your previous runs of the 80-140 in a barrel and run your last cooking. Keep adding your makings to the barrel, stirring and checking it until you get the proof you want. Most times we made 97-100 proof. But this could be drunk as is, or if you wanted it much better, you put all of this finished shine back in the cooker and cook it again. This time it comes out at 170 proof and you let it run to about 150. Take this and put it in a barrel and mix well or spring water with it to get the proof down. It still makes about the same amount, three runs always made 22-23 gallons. REMEMBER NO YEAST WAS ADDED.

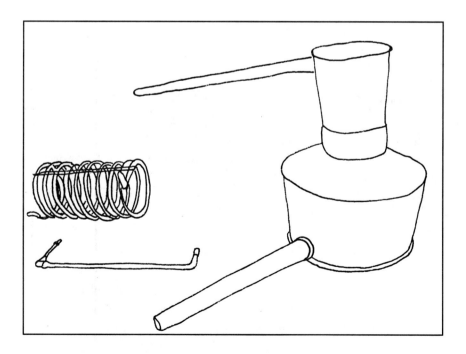

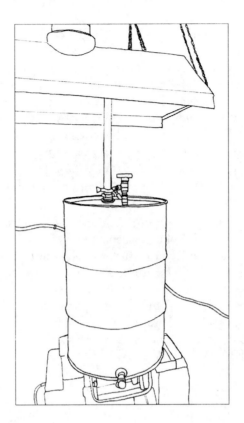

Afterward

The still illustration above is located at Flag Hill Farm in Vershire, VT. It's basically a 50-gallon stainless steel drum that is fired by propane. The apple farmer and distiller, Sebastian Lousada, distills Vermont brandy or "Calvados," what they call a "spirited essence of apples" or "Pomme-de-Vie." His brandy at the 2009 American Distilling Institute Brandy conference was considered by the judges to be one of the best in America.

A skilled distiller working with quality ingredients can produce a superior spirit on the most simple stills, in this case a 50-gallon drum.

We will soon see moonshine and whiskeys in the market place that push the boundary of the craft distillation to a new level. Their products will truly be "handcrafted" from local ingredients.

Answer Key

Chapter 1
1.) a
2.) d

Chapter 2
1.) b
2.) b
3.) c

Chapter 3
1.) d
2.) a

Chapter 4
1.) e

Chapter 5
1.) d
2.) b
3.) c
4.) b
5.) a
6.) c
7.) b

Chapter 6
1.) b
2.) a
3.) b
4.) c
5.) c
6.) a

Chapter 7
1.) e
2.) c

Chapter 8
1.) b
2.) a
3.) a
4.) c

Chapter 9
1.) b
2.) c
3.) a
4.) c

Chapter 10
1.) a
2.) b
3.) b
4.) c
5.) a
6.) c
7.) a
8.) b

Chapter 11
1.) b
2.) a
3.) b
4.) c
5.) c

6.) b
7.) a
8.) c
9.) b

CPSIA information can be obtained
at www.ICGtesting.com
Printed in the USA
FFOW01n1024311215
19736FF